D1825056

Testimonials

"*Self-awareness is one of the most important leadership traits nobody talks about. And yet it is absolutely critical for emotional intelligence. I Know Myself and Neither Do You is a must-read for anyone looking to propel their leadership skills to the next level.*" --**Emma Seppälä**, Associate Director for the Center for Compassion and Altruism, Research and Education, Stanford University School of Medicine; Co-Director of the Yale College Emotional Intelligence Project at the Yale Center for Emotional Intelligence; Faculty Director at the Yale School of Management's Leadership Program; and author of the best seller, The Happiness Track.

"*Ray Williams makes a compelling case for self-awareness as the key to leader success. Using in-depth research, case studies and personal insights, Williams shows how current and aspiring leaders can better understand themselves and improve their performance by recognizing the importance of self-awareness and taking action to improve it for the benefit of their team and organization. The book is a must have book on your reference shelf.*" -- **Marshall Goldsmith**, the only two-time Thinkers 50 #1 Leadership Thinker in the world and the New York Times #1 best-selling author of Triggers, Mojo, and What Got You Here Won't Get You There.

"*I Know Myself and Neither Do You is a wonderful compendium of research, thinking and tactics to help you improve your appreciation of self-awareness.*" – **Dan Pontefract**, Founder, Pontefract Group; keynote speaker; leadership strategist; and author of three best- selling books, including Lead. Care. Win. and Open to Think.

"One of the factors that holding back emerging, as well as veteran, leaders is a lack of self-awareness. This deficiency has nothing to do with intelligence. It comes with a reluctance to focus on self, which is natural because leaders are outwardly focused. *I Know Myself and Neither Do You* by Ray Williams can provide the insights leaders need to focus on in order to develop their self-awareness. The book offers real-world advice on developing your inner self through reflection and other means. *I Know Myself and Neither Do You* is a book leaders will want to read now and keep on the shelf for future reference."-- **John Baldoni**, 2019 Global Gurus Top 20; Inc.com Top 50 Leadership Expert; one of Marshall Goldsmith Top 100 Coaches; and author of many books on leadership, including GRACE: A Leader's Guide to a Better Us.

"*I Know Myself and Neither Do You* explains various aspects of self-awareness with striking stories and offers tools and techniques for leaders to develop their self-awareness. It elaborates emotional intelligence and mindfulness. It is an inspiring book on life leadership with examples and anecdotes. It appends with exercises including self-awareness assessment and mindfulness assessment for readers to assess themselves. I strongly recommend reading it!"— **Professor M. S. Rao**, #1 Thought Leader and Influencer on Culture Globally by Thinkers 360 and author of over 45 books including 21 Success Sutras for CEOs.

"In *I Know Myself and Neither Do You*, Ray Williams argues that a lack of leader self-awareness is the key to failure or success. Ray provides an in-depth examination of the historical and psychological elements of both internal and external self-awareness, with examples of how the key attribute can elevate leadership to greatness. The book gives the reader concrete strategies and tools on how leaders can raise their self-awareness." --**Dan Schawbel**, a New York Times bestselling author and the Managing Partner of Workplace Intelligence, and bestselling author of Back to Human: How Great Leaders Create Connection in the Age of Isolation, a Washington Post bestseller.

*"Ray Williams gives a well-researched, insightful guide to self-awareness and the skills leaders need today to thrive in their roles in his new book, **I Know Myself and Neither Do You.** His years of experience are shown on every page and there is something to take away in every chapter. This book is perfect for modern leaders looking to better understand themselves, top leadership qualities and how to lead an effective team as a result."* —**Eric Teruende**, Co-Founder, NoW of Work, International Speaker (250+ stages,) bestselling author of Rethink Work.

"In **I Know Myself and Neither Do You**, Ray Williams gives us a detailed examination of the critical importance of self-awareness for current and aspiring leaders, referencing the psychological, neuroscience and historical research on self-awareness and the value of self-reflection and solitude. Ray provides two case studies from his coaching experience, illustrating leaders with contrasting insufficient and enhanced self-awareness. The book is a valuable reminder of the central feature of good leadership is self-awareness and gives us invaluable strategies and tips on how to improve it." --**Maninder Dhaliwal,** ICD.D, President and CEO of Lions Gate International.

"Ray Williams gets to the core of how to be a successful leader. Well written and easy to follow and understand the meaning of how win-win leadership can be accomplished in today's demanding workplace." —**Alan Levy**, BA, MIR, LLM, Associate Professor, Brandon University, and mediator and arbitrator Canada wide.

I Know Myself and Neither Do You

Why Charisma, Confidence and Pedigree
Won't Take You Where You Want to Go

Ray Williams

Copyright © 2020 Ray Williams

All rights reserved.

No part of this publication may be reproduced, distributed, or transmitted in any form or by any means, including photocopying, recording, or other electronic or mechanical methods, without the prior written permission of the author, except in the case of brief cited quotations embodied in critical reviews and certain ether non-commercial uses permitted by copyright law.

Library of Congress Control Number: 2020907300

I know myself and neither do you: why charisma, confidence and pedigree won't take you where you want to go /by Ray Williams

Includes bibliographical references.

Amazon ISBN: 9798636052487

1. Self-awareness. 2. Know thyself

Note: The names, details and circumstances may have been changed to protect the privacy of those mentioned in this publication. This publication is not intended as a substitute for the advice of health care individuals.

Dedication

For my wife, partner and friend,

Diane, in gratitude for her

inspiration and never-ending support.

And for my father, Brinley Williams, a man of
exquisite integrity and honor and a shining
example of a master of himself.

Acknowledgements

Diane Williams, my wife, has edited this book several times and provided incisive and valuable direction and advice in addition to her unwavering support for this endeavour.

Stephanie Frank, best-selling author, successful entrepreneur and long time invaluable friend helped me focus on the essence of my message and how to deliver it to my audience effectively.

Mike Desjardins, Founder and CEO of Virtus Inc., a Vancouver-based leadership training and coaching company, has provided insightful feedback both on his personal journey of self-awareness and on the impact of the contents of this book, and what it is trying to achieve.

Contents

Preface

"If you know the enemy and know yourself, you need not fear the result of a hundred battles. If you know yourself but not the enemy, for every victory gained you will also suffer a defeat. If you know neither the enemy nor yourself, you will succumb in every battle."

Sun Tzu, *The Art of War*

I wrote this book before the full impact of the Covid-19 virus hit us. The impact has produced devastating damage and changes to the way we work and socialize that will have far-reaching effects. The forced isolation has fuelled anxiety, fear, depression and grief. At the same time, physical distancing and isolation have presented us with opportunities to relate and work differently, and given us substantially more time for self-reflection and self-awareness.

A Personal Story

My father, Brinley Williams was a great man. He knew what was important in life and how to conduct himself honorably and with humility. He was deeply self-reflective and was the most self-aware person I have ever known. Brinley had a difficult and challenging life, yet he exuded a quiet, powerful confidence and stillness that had a calming effect on me an all those who knew him. I loved to hear his life stories about his childhood working in the coal mine in Wales, leaving home at the tender age of 14, and at the age of 16 (with his parents' blessing), joining the British Army and serving in the Middle East for eleven dangerous years.

He went on to work for the British Foreign Service and was stationed in Hong Kong starting in the early 1930's. Which is where he met my mother who had immigrated to Hong Kong from Mexico. My father, mother, sister and brother were taken prisoner by the Japanese upon their invasion in 1941, and spent the remainder of the WWII in Stanley Internment Camp.

My parents did not like to speak about their brutal experience in the camp, and as I had been born in the POW camp, one month before the end of the war, I had few memories to rely upon. I'm thankful to my older sister, who remembered those years and readily shared her painful memories with me.

Toward the end of his life, when I was a grown man, my father more readily shared life his story with me. One day, we walked together in his garden among the award-winning flowers that he loved so much.

He pulled a weed out of the garden by his feet as he talked. He told me how he had survived the childhood years in the coal mine in Wales, and desert warfare in the Middle East while in the British Army; and the Battle for Hong Kong; then the years in the Hong Kong POW camp and years of recuperation after. As he spoke of those times, it was clear to me it was his ability to go to a place of calmness, and stillness, separated from the chaos around him that enabled him to survive and help his family survive. He said he was able to go to that private and powerful place within him to reach his innermost thoughts and feelings, and that gave him the strength to go on living, to survive the worst.

Every day in the POW camp, he said, he would find a quiet corner of the camp after his duties for family were done, and quietly contemplate his inner feelings, and then focus on one thought-- "let's get through today." For almost four years he had to be a pillar of strength and calm and help his family deal with insufficient food, appalling conditions and protect them as much as he could from the brutality of the Japanese captors. His biggest test was when my mother miraculously became pregnant with me, but became very ill, and the camp doctor didn't think she or I would live. He had to tell my brother and sister than she might die. We both survived—barely.

In his retirement years, my father loved to spend quiet times in solitude, either reading fiction, working in the garden, painting or writing, or simply reflecting. It's not that he was anti-social or lonely. Indeed, he had spent his life in public service consistently interacting with others and his family. It's that he valued the time with himself for reflection.

Brinley Williams was keenly aware of his emotions and the impact he had on others. It was my experience with him that stimulated my interest in self-awareness and prompted me to make sincere efforts at self-mastery.

He knew who he was, and it was apparent in every word he spoke and action he took with great consistency. And this personal mastery gave him the skills and power to be more sensitive to and intuitive with other people, as well as emanate a great strength and resilience.

In contrast, so many leaders today lack that self-awareness.

Leadership is in crisis today. Leaders in organizations and institutions worldwide have failed to deliver on their promises, inspire people and initiate changes to improve people's well-being and that of our planet. In poll after survey, trust in our leaders is at an all-time low. In both government and business, media stories abound about corruption and wrong doing. All too often leaders act out of self-interest, blind to the welfare of others. The result often is political and social unrest, and declining productivity and well-being in the workplace.

Many observers and pundits have given explanations for the current negative state, ranging from the negative impact of technology to increasing polarization and tribalism of the population and income inequality, but many of those factors are external to the inner workings of people, and the solutions offered are often external as well. Rarely do the pundits look inside.

This book looks inside the minds and hearts of leaders as a perspective and strategy that could change the culture of organizations and address the issues identified above. I suggest that the development of greater self-awareness by leaders can be a powerful way of improving our working lives, and perhaps also our personal lives.

I argue that leader self-awareness as a core foundational piece of emotional intelligence has been relatively ignored as a leadership and organizational strategy, yet the benefits and positive impact can be significant.

Part of that strategy would be a shift from leader self-interest and focus on external things to a greater focus on a leader's thoughts, and emotions, which in turn impact the leader's decisions and actions.

Allied to this shift is the need for leaders to embrace solitude and quiet reflection time, which aids in self-awareness to improve the quality of their decisions, ideas and relationships.

This book describes the research on self-awareness and also outlines specific activities that leaders can engage in to improve their self-awareness. The book is a natural progression from my previous book, *Eye of the Storm: How Mindful Leaders Can Transform Chaotic Workplaces,* which examines in detail the benefits of mindfulness practices for leaders and the workplace.

The following is an example of a leader who struggled with self-awareness, with unfortunate results for him. I will call him Robert.

He sat behind his large desk and gazed out the floor to ceiling window at the city of skyscrapers. Behind him was a large screen TV tuned into CNBC. On his desk was an active computer, and in front of him on the desk was a large smartphone, with the active screen face up.

He was the CEO of a large company that was going through the process of reorganization and repositioning in the marketplace. His Board had recommended he engage an executive coach.

He called me.

Our first meeting was a revelation of his lack of self-control and egotism.

"I'm pissed off that we're not getting the results my team had committed to," he exclaimed in a loud voice, slamming his hand on the desk, "I made a commitment to the Board, and they'll hold me responsible."

As yet, we hadn't talked about what he hoped to accomplish with our coaching arrangement or an agenda for our first meeting.

"You're angry," I said calmly.

"Wouldn't you be too," he snapped, "if some people on your executive team were lazy or incompetent, or disloyal?" He turned and glanced at the stock market screen behind him and then glanced at the face of his smart-phone on his desk.

"How does that make you angry?" I inquired.

"The board expects results, and the hell if I'm going to take the fall for others' failures," he answered vehemently.

"So you're angry because the board is holding you accountable or because others won't be blamed for failure?"

He stared at me for a moment, but said nothing.

"So what's the outcome you want here?" I asked.

"It's obvious, isn't it? I want my team to produce results and fast. I made that abundantly clear."

A notification on his phone lit up and he picked it up to read, then looked at me with critical eyes.

Directly, I asked, "Is it possible you could be part of the problem?"

He laughed, glancing at his phone, and then his watch. "Get serious, Ray. And just a reminder, you're here to help me strategize ways to get my term functioning effectively. I'm not the problem."

This was not going to go well for Robert, I thought. "So what other emotions are you feeling right now about the situation?" I asked.

"My feelings have nothing to do with it. It's obvious that I have a problem in some team members lacking the skills and attitude to do what is necessary."

"What kinds of things might you do to motivate them to perform better?" I inquired.

"The only motivation they need is the threat of losing their jobs," he replied, half laughing.

Glancing again up at the TV screen, then down to his watch, he added, "I've got to run to another meeting. Thanks for listening to my problem."

And at that, he stood up, signalling the session was over.

As I was leaving, I said in an even tone, "Reflect on the questions I asked you today when you have some quiet alone time. And at our next meeting, let's set some outcomes for our coaching process."

He sighed, "Sure, if I get some time."

I knew he would never get the time, and definitely would not get what he wanted from his organization. Despite his overconfidence and arrogance, his self-awareness was seriously impaired.

You'll read more about Robert and what happened to him later in the book.

I've had this kind of conversation with varying degrees of seriousness with more than a few senior executives during my 35 years of working with leaders. It is reflective of a phenomenon all too commonplace in our organizations, where leaders see their organization's problems as someone else's fault. These leaders often exhibit a serious lack of self-awareness and the negative impact they have on others. And the results are often detrimental to the organization and ultimately the leader.

Along with this lack of self-awareness were the signs and behaviors of a fragmented way of working, which affected their ability to focus, and increased levels of stress, which included a constant and continual race to keep up to the e-mails, text messages, meetings, phone messages and conversations, with no time for reflection, and virtually no attempt at gathering their thoughts in solitude and quiet.

The workplace and job of leadership has changed. Traditional organizational structures, bureaucratic practices, and leader recruitment and promotion are still common in many of our institutions. Yet automation, a global economy, and the values of the younger generations are challenging these traditional structures and practices.

The successful leaders I've had the privilege of working with have developed rigorous habits which promote and enhance self-awareness and make them more effective and help them to rise to greatness. This book identifies, describes and promotes the importance of the process of "inside-out"-- the mastery of self, and incisive self-awareness that becomes the major stepping stone to great leadership.

Great leaders resonate with others because they know themselves and are attuned to what others think and feel. Learning how to be more aware of the perceptions of others is a skill set that will benefit those who seek to be more effective as leaders or in any relationship. By understanding more about ourselves and our unconscious tendencies to self-deceive, we can improve our ability to build relationships, strengthen organizations, and confront the fears that cause us to live beneath our potential. Self-examination is a preparation for insight, a groundbreaking for the seeds of self-understanding which gradually bloom into changed behavior.

Great leaders have also recognized the importance of regularly seeking out quiet solitude and stillness to allow the brain to integrate a cascade of the thoughts and feelings that inundate them on a daily basis, understanding also that these quiet times can be a source of creativity.

Making the commitment to explore the inner reaches of our hearts and minds allows us to be true to ourselves and enables us to honor the duties we owe to self, others, and the society in which we live.

Now, more than ever, leaders in organizations need to raise their self-awareness both internally so that they are truly connected to their inner emotions, thoughts and perceptions, and externally, to see themselves as others see them, so that they can more accurately assess the impact they are making on others and the world.

Leaders require elevated self-awareness, self-reflection and the habit of seeking out quiet solitude to become great leaders in their organizations and communities.

It is my hope that this book can be a valuable resource for leaders, leadership trainers, consultants and coaches searching for ways leaders can be more successful, and fulfilled in their work.

I Know Myself and Neither Do You

Introduction

"Each man had only one genuine vocation-to find the way to himself...His task was to discover his own destiny-not an arbitrary one-and to live it out wholly and resolutely within himself."

Herman Hesse

Today, there are multiple signs that organizations are exhibiting the signs of dysfunction and decay with a detrimental impact on the people who work there. This disturbing picture is punctuated by the absence and dysfunctions of leaders in our organizations and institutions. The result is chaos and unhealthy workplaces.

A contributing force to this disturbing situation is the lack of self-awareness of our leaders, along with our under appreciation of its importance.

A study by the non-profit Families and Work Institute showed that one in three American employees are chronically overworked. According to the U.S. National Institute for Occupational Safety, stress-related ailments cost companies $200-$300 billion annually. And 70-90% of employee hospital visits are linked to stress. Azagba and Mesbah Sharaf of the Department of Economics at Concordia University concluded that health care expenditures for employees with high levels of stress were 46% greater than at similar organizations without high levels of stress.

Today, the average worker works more hours per week than in 2000, and 37% of the population say they work on their vacation.

The most recent poll by Weber Shandwick reported that 65% of Americans say the lack of civility is a major problem that has worsened since the financial crisis and recession. What's even more distressing is that nearly 50% of those surveyed said they were withdrawing from the basic tenants of democracy—government and politics—because of incivility and bullying.

In two surveys by the Workplace Bullying Institute (WBI) and Zogby International, where bullying was defined as "repeated mistreatment: Sabotage by others that prevented work from getting done, verbal abuse, threatening conduct, intimidation and humiliation." And 35% of workers experienced bullying first hand, and 62% of the bullies were men. A Harris Interactive poll conducted in 2011 revealed that 34% of women reported being bullied in the workplace. A *U.S. News and World Report* poll says that 89% of U.S. workers said incivility is a serious problem and 78% said it is getting worse.

The Conference Board of Canada's study, "Building Healthy Workplaces," estimates that 44% of Canadians say they've coped with a mental health problem such as extreme stress, substance abuse, schizophrenia, depression, burnout and addictions. The report went on to state that almost 50% of managers had no training in managing workers with mental health issues.

Research conducted in the past decade has shown that employee engagement has declined significantly in most industries, with some research citing as few as 29% of employees being actively engaged in their jobs.

Reports of "toxic workplaces" and "toxic bosses" proliferate news and social media stories, where a significant number of employees want to leave their jobs because of abusive bosses. In *The Corporation*, the hit 2003 documentary film, businesses are portrayed as psychopaths that can wreak havoc in the communities where they operate, something that is becoming increasingly commonplace.

Relentless demands, extreme pressure and ruthlessness are all trademarks of a toxic company, as is a twisted disconnect between what a firm says it does for employees and what it actually is doing. People are looked at as costs, rather than assets.

All these descriptions of dysfunctional and unhealthy organizations have been contrasted with progressive organizations and their leaders, who understand and value the well-being of employees as central to the long-term success of the organization.

The World Economic Forum's 2015 Survey on the Global Agenda revealed that 86% of respondents perceive a global crisis in leadership. The survey assessed the general concerns and issues about leadership, not the specific issue of leadership during a crisis. That deficiency is more disconcerting in the face of increasing global social, political and economic complexities and now, pandemics.

A study by Deloitte's Center for the Edge shows that the effectiveness of management in organizations has been steadily falling for the last 50 years.

In the past two decades, 30% of Fortune 500 CEOs have lasted less than 3 years. Top executive failure rates are as high as 75% and rarely less than 30%. Chief executives now are lasting 7.6 years on a global average down from 9.5 years in 1995. According to the

Harvard Business Review, 2 out of 5 new CEOs fail in their first 18 months on the job.

According to the *National Leadership Index report*, 75% of organizations reported a deficit of leadership skills. Forty-two per cent of managers rate their own line-manager as ineffective; 70% of Americans still believe they have a crisis of leadership.

A 2016 Gallup poll found that only 18% of managers demonstrate a high level of talent for managing others--meaning a shocking 82% of managers aren't very good at leading people. Gallup estimated that this lack of leadership capability costs U.S. corporations up to $550 billion annually.

In a 2016 McKinsey & Company study of more than 52,000 managers and employees, leaders rated themselves as better and more engaging than their employees did. This included 86% of leaders who believed they model the improvements they want employees to make, while another 77% of leaders believed they "inspire action."

Research shows when someone assumes a new or different leadership role they have a 40% chance of demonstrating disappointing performance. Furthermore, 82% of newly appointed leaders derail because they fail to build partnerships with subordinates and peers. Public poll after public poll has shown that people have lost confidence in our political and business leaders.

A study by the Corporate Leadership Council concluded that the billions upon billions of dollars spent on leadership training have improved productivity by only 2%.

It appears that the major reason for the failure has nothing to do with technical competence, or knowledge, or experience, but rather with hubris and ego, most often linked to a lack of emotional intelligence and particularly, self-awareness.

Leigh Branham, author of *7 Hidden Reasons Employees Leave*, analyzed over 20,000 anonymous surveys asking employees why they left their last job. Although most managers believe pay is the primary reason people quit, Branham discovered that the number one reason actually is "loss of trust and confidence in senior leaders," and that loss of trust is often correlated to abusive or narcissistic bosses.

Psychologist and researcher Amy Brunell of Ohio State University has studied leadership and expresses concern about the prevalence of narcissism in leadership positions. Her study, published in the journal *Personality and Social Psychology*, comes from a study of business managers. She says, "Narcissists have an inflated view of their talents and abilities and are all about themselves," adding, "It's not surprising that narcissists become leaders. They like power. They are egotistical, and they are usually charming and extraverted. The problem is they don't necessarily make better leaders."

In their book, *Snakes in Suits: When Psychopaths Go to Work*, Paul Babiak and Robert Hare argue while psychopaths may not be ideally suited for traditional work environments by virtue of a lack of desire to develop good interpersonal relationships, they have other abilities such as reading people and masterful influence and persuasion skills that can make it difficult to see them as the psychopaths they are. According to their and others' studies, up to 25% of executives could be assessed as psychopaths, a much higher figure than the general population figure of 1%.

Manifred Kets de Vries, a distinguished Clinical Professor of Leadership Development and Organizational Change at INSEAD describes the corporate psychopath the "SOB —Seductive Operational Bully." SOBs don't usually end up in jail or psychiatric hospital but they do thrive in an organizational setting. SOBs can be found wherever power, status, or money is at stake, de Vries says.

David Dotlich and Peter C. Cairo, in their book, *Why CEOs Fail: The 11 Behaviors That Can Derail Your Climb to the Top and How to Manage Them,* present 11 cogent reasons why CEOs fail, most of which have to do with hubris, ego and a lack of emotional intelligence.

Tomas Chamorro-Premuzic, chief talent scientist at Manpower Group, a professor of business psychology at University College London and at Columbia University in New York City, an associate at Harvard's Entrepreneurial Finance Lab and author of the book *Why Do So Many Incompetent Men Become Leaders? (and How to Fix It),* asks the question and provides an answer "Have you ever worked with people who are not as good as they think they are ... men are typically more deceived about their talents than women are. And they are also more likely to succeed in their careers. That's because one of the best ways to fool other people into thinking you're better than you actually are is to fool yourself first."

Chamorrow-Premuzic asserts his research shows that so many men are incompetent because of these reasons: "First, we fail to distinguish between confidence and competence, and men are universally over-confident; the second reason is our love for charismatic individuals, fuelled by mass media; and the third reason is our inability to resist the allure of narcissistic individuals."

The result? Many leaders who are "unaware of their limitations and unjustifiably pleased with themselves, Chamorrow-Premuzic says, "They see leadership as an entitlement and they lack empathy and self-control, so they end up acting without integrity and indulging in reckless risks."

Ron Carucci, writing in the *Harvard Business Review*, describes the failures of modern leadership: "The pattern is clear, and diligent leaders often devote countless resources to planning out the perfect change management initiative. To raise the odds of success, however, my experience suggests the place that leaders need to begin their transformation efforts is not their organizations: It's themselves."

All of this research and expert perspectives underscore the lack of and need for leaders with emotional intelligence, and enhanced self-awareness. We need leaders whose orientation is primarily inside-out, being grounded in their inner selves, and keenly aware of how others view them. We need leaders who are the masters of themselves first, before aspiring to be the masters of anyone else.

In the following chapters I provide a detailed look at self-awareness, self-reflection, including the negative and positive impacts of self-awareness by leaders, with suggestions on how self-awareness can be developed. I describe in detail the supporting elements of mindfulness, solitude and quiet which strengthen and expand the capacity for self-awareness. And finally, I provide both specific self-awareness and mindfulness assessments and activities that can assist readers in developing further their self-awareness.

This book is not about a return to some magical time in the past, where leadership was simple or straightforward. We can never return to the past.

This book is about seeing, recruiting, promoting, and believing in leaders who have focused on self-mastery, rather than the mastery of the external environment and things. It's about the power of self-awareness, self-reflection, mindfulness, and solitude that can powerfully connect with people to create a better present and better future for all of us.

1

A Self-Awareness Tale of Robert and Daniel

"It is absurd that a man should rule others, who cannot rule himself."

Latin Proverb

To illustrate how important self-awareness is for leaders, I provide a contrasting description of two leaders I coached who had very different experiences and success. Their names have been changed to protect confidentiality.

Robert

Robert was a CEO of a large company that was financially profitable when his predecessor retired after 10 years at the helm.

The Board of Directors, in its wisdom, had made a condition of Robert's appointment the requirement that he work with an executive coach. They hired an experienced coach who worked with Robert for 6 months, before by mutual agreement, they terminated the arrangement. Robert did not engage another coach for almost two years.

Then one day the Chairman of the Board of the company contacted me and asked if I'd be interested in working with Robert.

We had a good extensive discussion during which he expressed concern about reports he had been getting from employees about Robert's leadership style, and behaviors. He suggested I meet with Robert and see if the two of us would be agreeable to working together. I said that I would, and I set up a meeting with Robert a week later.

Before meeting Robert, I gleaned as much information as I could about his background and experience.

When I first met Robert in his office, I was struck by some immediate impressions. First, he was a physically imposing man in his early 40s--tall, handsome, with a palatable energy of confidence and command. He had a business degree and MBA, but had not distinguished himself as a student. While involved in his MBA program, he had also been working as an entrepreneur, creating a start-up which had created a business tool app for busy executives. The company was successful, and within three years was bought out by a large corporation. In many ways Robert was a stereotypical leader of a Silicon Valley company--brash, aggressive, bold and creative.

As I came to learn in the ensuing months, he was clearly driven, impatient, intolerant of others and insensitive to their feelings. His rapid-fire manner of speaking, almost in bullet points, was a reflection of his style.

As I was to find out, Robert had a small loyal core of supporters, some of whom idolized him, and others who supported and tolerated him for personal gain, and then there was a much larger group of employees, colleagues and others who disliked and distrusted Robert.

When Robert first arrived at the company, he quickly made drastic strategic, organization and personnel changes.

Theses changes had produced some immediate successes, and on the other hand, had alienated a significant number of employees, some of whom showed their displeasure by leaving the company.

When confronted with the negative feedback, Robert's response was that the only measure that he or the Board cared about was the bottom-line performance for shareholders, and in that, he was successful.

Quickly his intemperate reputation spread, and the kind of people he attracted both in his personal and business lives tended to be those whose prime motive was either self-interest, or an "ends-justifies-the-means" philosophy. Robert was idolized by his fans for his success or feared by his competitors for his ruthlessness.

In our initial coaching sessions, Robert quickly tried to establish dominance and take control of the sessions, as he did with most relationships. I had been around enough other executives with similar behaviour patterns to recognize that I had to challenge him immediately. I confronted him about his attempts, indicating that if our relationship was not to be one of equals, I would withdraw from the coaching arrangement. That response seemed to gain credibility with him, and he modified his behaviour accordingly, although, like all bad habits, he couldn't resist lapsing back into this default behaviour occasionally.

In a rare moment of self-insight, he confessed he was unhappy, and never seemed to be satisfied with his success (which partially explains his workaholism). In addition, Robert confessed that he knew others disliked or feared him, and he wished he had closer meaningful relationships. During one rare moment in our coaching sessions, Robert admitted that he wanted to change, but was concerned that his admission of needing to change would be seen by others as weakness.

It was clear to me that one of the major problems Robert had was his lack of self-awareness, and that was having a significant negative impact on others. We agreed that we would spend some considerable time talking about this and what could be done.

In the first few coaching sessions we had, he started to become more open to the importance of raising his self-awareness, emotional intelligence and more open to the value of feedback from others. In a rare moment of vulnerability and honesty with himself and me, he admitted that sometimes he felt he was a fraud, and he was deathly afraid of being "found out" for being a fraud and phony. I asked him if he was okay about that observation and did he want to do anything about it. I felt here was an opening where he could commit to change. Then in an instant, the look of vulnerability on his face was gone, and he returned to his usual overconfident and guarded projected persona.

I was still optimistic that together we could return to that place of his vulnerability and openness, and that we could begin a discussion about making some small changes. It was not to be.

It was not difficult to feel empathy and compassion for Robert. He had spent his professional life (and much of his personal life) focused on the external manifestations of his identity--financial rewards, an affluent lifestyle, and basking in the limelight--and yet at the same time was so out of touch with his inner state. His

4

carefully crafted outer identity had become his inner identity. Yet, there were the undercurrents of sadness, unhappiness, and a yearning to reveal his real self.

Robert never had a chance to try to make the changes he needed in his life; he suffered a massive heart attack and died. At his funeral, there were only his family and a couple of friends, and very few people from his business life. Sitting at his funeral service, I reflected on his inability to take the opportunity to become more fully self-aware and feel real personal fulfillment and happiness. It was tragic.

Daniel

Daniel is a C-Suite Executive in his mid-50s in a large international manufacturing company. He had varied experiences in different industries including the financial services sector in an HR capacity, but had been promoted into operations with wide-ranging responsibilities including the key advisor to the CEO.

His personal life was as important as his work life, as was evident from him limiting his work hours and putting his family first over work. In addition, Daniel had a wide circle of friends that he had known for many years, and he was also actively involved in the community.

Daniel had engaged me as his coach while he was at his previous company, and when he joined the manufacturing company, he asked me to continue to work with him and I agreed.

While Daniel's technical and organizational skills are outstanding, he was known for the strength of his interpersonal relationships with employees, peers and colleagues and business associates. While Daniel's warm and open personality was a big contributor to his success, he has intentionally engaged in behaviors that have augmented his emotional intelligence, including engaging a coach, regularly taking time to reflect on his inner state and emotions, and taking action on 360 assessments where there was a gap between others' and his own perceptions.

As a result, the trust level personal commitment that Daniel enjoyed with others was very high. He was always thinking and acting upon those thoughts about how to empower, enable and support his people. A secondary result is that Daniel's reputation travelled far beyond his company, so that he became a very desirable talent in the executive workplace, and was approached several times by recruitment head-hunters for other positions.

During our coaching sessions, Daniel was open to any tool or practice that would increase his self-awareness, and engaged in a program of regular reflection time, solitude retreats and "doing nothing" to enhance his creativity.

Daniel had already engaged in considerable work to raise his self-awareness, both with me and on his own. Our sessions, assessments and personal goals continued to enhance his willingness to see his blind spots, be vulnerable, and relate to his employees and colleagues with compassion, kindness and empathy.

2

What is Self-Awareness and Why Does It Matter?

"Without reflection, we go blindly on our way, creating more unintended consequences, and failing to achieve anything useful."

Margaret J. Wheatley

Defining Self-Awareness

Self-awareness can be defined as an awareness of one's own personality, character or individuality. Psychologist Daniel Goleman proposed a popular definition of self-awareness in his best-selling book *Emotional Intelligence: Why It Can Matter More Than IQ*, as "knowing one's internal states, preference, resources, and intuitions."

Other phrases and words are often used to mean self-awareness:

- Self-reflection has also been referred to at various times as "self-consciousness," "introspection," or "self-awareness," all having slightly different connotations but emphasizing the same concept. Self-reflection is careful thought about your own behavior and beliefs and involves self-examination, self-observation, and soul-searching.

- Self-consciousness can be defined as being conscious of one's own acts or states as belonging to or originating in oneself; aware of oneself as an individual.
- Introspection can be defined as observation or examination of one's own mental and emotional state, mental process; the act of looking within oneself.
- Self-knowledge can be defined as an understanding of oneself or one's own motives or character.

All the definitions suggest an examination of one's internal thoughts and feelings and reflecting on what they mean. This process can be focused on either one's current or past mental experiences.

Beyond the ability to be reflectively aware of oneself, self-awareness is often associated with executive processes in the brain essential to the self-regulation of emotions. Thus, the self-aware individual is often viewed as more controlled and intentional.

Why Does Self-Awareness Matter?

In 1972, psychologists Shelley Duval and Robert Wicklund published their theory of self-awareness, which argued "when we focus our attention on ourselves, we evaluate and compare our current behavior to our internal standards and values. We become self-conscious as objective evaluators of ourselves." Duval and Wicklund believe self-awareness was a major mechanism of self-control.

In his paper, "How Self-Awareness Impacts Your Work, " Daniel Goleman argues the ability to monitor our emotions and thoughts from moment to moment is a key to understanding ourselves better, being at peace with whom we are and proactively managing our thoughts, emotions and behaviors.

People who are self-aware act intentionally and consciously rather than reactively or passively, Goleman contends. They also have an elevated sensitivity to the impact their words and behavior have on others.

According to researcher Matthew Lippincott, "Developing Emotional Self-Awareness is a crucial first step in effective leadership because it lays the foundation upon which the other eleven Emotional and Social Intelligence Competencies are built. We can't develop skills like Emotional Self-Control, Empathy, or Teamwork unless we are coming from a place of Emotional Self-Awareness. It gives leaders the necessary information about themselves and the effectiveness of their interactions so that they can monitor their emotions and manage their behaviors accordingly."

Executive coaches often deal with difficult clients, particularly executives who tend to be overconfident and arrogant. It's been my experience that the most difficult to deal with and coach are the leaders who lack self-awareness. They are either unaware of their inner state and how others view them, or they are aware and they don't care about other's perceptions.

Self-aware people recognize about their limitations and strengths, and they will welcome constructive feedback from others. In contrast, people with low self-awareness may respond to critical feedback as a threat or sign of failure.

It's clear that self-awareness is foundational to emotional intelligence and is critical to our ability to communicate effectively with and build relationships of trust with others. Individuals high in self-awareness are skilled at self-monitoring and in adapting their behaviors to relate effectively with others.

Many important studies show that self-awareness is not a strong trait for many leaders, particularly male leaders. While women in executive-level management positions tend to exhibit more self-awareness than men in the same positions, the overall percentages suggest there is much opportunity for growth in this area. In a study of 17,000 individuals worldwide, the Hay Group Research found that 19 percent of women executives interviewed exhibited self-awareness as compared to 4 percent of their male counterparts.

According to Tasha Eurich, writing in the *Harvard Business Review*, "research suggests that when we see ourselves clearly, we are more confident and more creative. We make sounder decisions, build stronger relationships, and communicate more effectively. We're less likely to lie, cheat, and steal. We are better workers who get more promotions. And we're more effective leaders with more satisfied employees and more profitable companies."

One of the effects of increased self-awareness is emotional intensity. Focusing on one's emotions or physiological responses amplifies one's subjective experience. Self-awareness also increases accurate access to one's self-concept. Self-regulation, a tangential component of self-awareness, increases our ability smoothly navigate our social environment through the self-regulation of our emotions, which includes altering one's behavioral, resisting temptation, changing one's mood, and selecting a response from various options.

One of the most significant observations that I made over a thirty-plus year period of training, coaching and mentoring leaders in small and large organizations is the degree to which self-awareness was not identified as an important element in providing feedback to leaders and the surprising number of experienced leaders in organizations who both undervalued and lacked sufficient self-awareness.

3

Self-Awareness Through the Ages

"Man know thyself; then thou shalt know the Universe and God."

Pythagoras

Although it is occasionally suggested that a concern with self-awareness as a result of self-reflection is a peculiarly modern phenomenon, originating with the French mathematician Descartes ("I think, therefore I am"), it is in fact the topic of lively ancient and medieval debates, many of which prefigure early modern and contemporary concerns.

As I read about the wisdom of ancient philosophers and leaders, I was struck by the almost universal belief they had about the importance of self-knowledge and self-awareness as the foundation for proper action and behavior.

The phrase *"nosce te ipsum,"* or "know thyself" has been an ageless theme throughout history, reflected in the writings of great thinkers such as Socrates, Ovid, Cicero, in the sayings of the Seven Sages of Greece, in early Christian writings, in Vedic literature, and in Taoist texts.

Legends tell us that the seven sages of ancient Greece who laid the foundation for western culture, gathered together in Delphi and encapsulated their wisdom into this expression. It was subsequently attributed to a dozen other authors, of which Thales of Miletus most commonly takes the honor.

The ancient Greek playwright Aeschylus used the maxim "know thyself" in his play *Prometheus Bound,* in which Prometheus bemoans the injustice of having been bound to a cliff side by Zeus, king of the Olympian gods. The demi-god Oceanus visits Prometheus and admonishes him to "know thyself" before he blames others.

Socrates' student Plato expressed the idea of "Know Thyself" extensively through the words of Socrates. In Plato's *Charmides,* and *Protagoras,* Socrates engages in a long dialogue about how we may gain knowledge of ourselves. In Plato's *Philebus* dialogue, Socrates refers back to the same usage of "know thyself" to build an example of the ridiculous for Protarchus. Socrates says in *Phaedrus,* that people make themselves appear ridiculous when they are trying to know obscure things before they know themselves.

Plato also argues understanding oneself enables one to understand others. In Plato's Socratic dialogue *Apology,* Socrates declares "the unexamined life is not worth living", that wisdom is only attainable through solitary introspection without the influence of others.

The Stoic philosophers discussed and wrote extensively about the self-examined life. Their recipe for evolving self-awareness included being suspicious about one's own perceptions and opinions of events until they were tested, and secondly, taking an opposite approach with evaluating the behavior of others--for example, being sympathetic before being suspicious.

Despite the commonly held belief that the idea of self-awareness originated with the Greeks, it may have originated from other ancient cultures. Evidence exists, for example, from the Coffin Texts of ancient Egypt in 2000 B.C. Other evidence shows an even earlier origin back to 3000 B.C. from the Old Kingdom Egyptian dynasties, which would predate the Hindu Vedas, the Greek philosophers and the Chinese I-Ching. Hindu scriptures focus on self-awareness as a way of attaining immortality. The Hindu Upanishads argue man is not born with self-awareness, so it becomes a lifelong challenge.

In 89 B.C., the Chinese emperor Wu released the Repenting Edict of Luntai, to apologize publically to his people about his past policy mistakes. Shortly after the release of the Edict, he ceased wars and territorial expansion and promoted agriculture, and other public benefit initiatives, which set the foundation for the successful reign of the Han Dynasty for more than 300 years. Wu has been ranked as one of the most successful emperors in Chinese history and had a reputation for being a reflective and self-aware leader.

Self-Awareness Wisdom Since the Middle Ages

The Romans adopted "Know Thyself" from the Greeks, and the Latin translation, *nosce te ipsum*, became a common western adage.

The Platonic tradition continued through the influence of St. Augustine and is associated with the view that the mind "gains the knowledge of [itself] through itself." Thus, self-awareness requires no awareness of the external world. St. Thomas Aquinas, writing in the thirteenth century, synthesized Platonic and Aristotelian thought by claiming that there is a form of self-awareness--awareness that one exists--for which, "the mere presence of the mind suffices."

In 1651, the 17th century English philosopher Thomas Hobbes used the term *nosce te ipsum* which he translated as "read thyself" in his famous work, *The Leviathan*. He asserted that one learns more by studying oneself, particularly the feelings that influence our thoughts and motivate our actions. In 1734, English poet Alexander Pope's poem "An Essay on Man, Epistle II", expresses the concept in the lines "Know then thyself, presume not God to scan, the proper study of mankind is Man." In 1750, American political leader Benjamin Franklin's *Poor Richard's Almanac,* claimed "There are three Things extremely hard, Steel, a Diamond, and to know one's self." In 1754, French philosopher Jean-Jacques Rousseau in his *Discourse on the Origin of Inequality* emphasized the importance of the inscription of the Temple at Delphi.

In 1831, American literary great Ralph Waldo Emerson wrote a poem entitled "Know Thyself" which focused on knowing the "God" within each person. In 1832, English writer Samuel T. Coleridge wrote a poem entitled "Self Knowledge" in which the text centers on the Delphic maxim "Know Thyself."

"Know Thyself" has subsequently appeared in many literary works, from Shakespearian theatre and Sufi literature. The concept of self-awareness also appears in the eighteenth century with American poet Walt Whitman.

Physician and philosopher Wilhelm Wundt expanded on the idea of self-awareness in the late 1800s. Borrowing on some Buddhist concepts, Wundt focused on three areas of mental functioning: thoughts, images, and feelings. He emphasized the importance of the internal processes of reflection and emotions.

In more recent times in the movie medium, the moviemakers Wachowski brothers used another Latin version of "know thyself" –

"*temet nosce*"--as an inscription over the Oracle's door in their movies *The Matrix* and *The Matrix Revolutions*. The transgender character Nomi in the Netflix show *Sense8,* also directed by the Wachowskis, has a tattoo on her arm with the Greek version of the phrase. "Know Thyself."

4

Core Beliefs, Values and Self-Identity

"There are three methods to gaining wisdom. The first is reflection, which is the highest. The second is imitation, which is the easiest. The third is experience, which is the bitterest."

Confucius

Examining Our Core Beliefs

To live a meaningful life where our values and beliefs are in alignment with our actions, we need to reflect upon our core beliefs on a regular basis. This process also helps us deal with the problem of self-deception. A classic definition of self-deception is that an individual "believes in two contradictory beliefs" at the same time without acknowledging that a conflict exists. The challenge in knowing ourselves is our willingness to engage "in objective self-examination and also accepting whatever personal shortcomings" that may be uncovered by that self-examination process.

Our willingness to conduct a self-examination requires both confidence and humility. And it allows us to more accurately assess the gap between self-assessment and the evaluations of others.

Researcher Lawrence Ackerman has identified the importance of clarifying and understanding our core beliefs and the undertaking of self-correcting action--including the vital process of understanding how we deceive ourselves.

He argues our ability to view accurately the world requires that we understand ourselves and our preconceived biases that cause us to distort reality. Self-identity, self-awareness, and self-deception all provide us with an opportunity to enrich our understanding of moral duties implicit in human relationships, Ackerman contends. Further, by understanding how identity, self-awareness, and self-deception apply within a business context, organizations can enhance relationships, build trust and commitment, and improve organizational outcomes.

What is the "Self?"

In psychology the self is often concerned with finding one's "true" self, expressed through self-coherence, self-identification and self-actualization. With a few notable exceptions (William James, neo-Freudians and humanists), psychologists largely ignored the self until the late 20th century. Only with the decline of behaviorism and psychoanalysis did the self emerge as a topic of consideration.

Philosophy, on the other hand, has a long history of examining the self. In the East, we have the *Upanishads*, the *Tao te Ching* and the teachings of Gautama Buddha. In the West, we had Plato followed by pre-Enlightenment religious philosophers who were concerned with the sinful qualities of the self. During the Enlightenment, various philosophers--Descartes, Locke, Hume, Leibnitz, Berkeley and Kant--wrote about the self. Ever since, philosophers have continually disagreed on the nature of the self, referring to "the problem of the self," which includes such questions as: Is there a self? How can we know it? What is the nature of the self in self-awareness? What does the self have to do with the brain?

In the West, abstract reflection has dominated since Descartes, separating subject and object, self and other, and self and the world of objects (this is often referred to as dualism).

In this tradition, the concept of the separate "I" entity is based on psychological structures or schemas. Accordingly, the development of a secure and strong ego became a goal in Western psychology.

In contrast, because of the influence of Eastern philosophy and religion, self-reflection is seen in the West as embodied, mindful and open to the ever-changing nature of bodily sensations that do not presume an independent self that engages in that reflection. Instead, the observer becomes one with the experience of reflection, and reflection becomes a form of experience itself. It is a fully embodied state of being, characterized by the awareness and acceptance of bodily sensation, non-attachment to "self-letting go and letting be." In this way, self-awareness is seen as a path for transformation and personal growth.

We have been conditioned to believe that our "self" is our thoughts and everything that lies beneath the surface of the skin. Yet, some would argue that it is only a small part in comparison to what is hidden. According to cognitive neuroscientists, the thoughts you consciously have throughout the day make up only 5% of cognitive activity. The other 95% of brain activity goes on beyond conscious awareness. To identify yourself simply from your conscious thoughts would be like predicting the end results of a math test with one hundred questions only after answering five.

Self-Awareness and Identity

At the personal or individual level, identity also encompasses those central, enduring, and distinctive attributes of an individual.

At the organizational level, identity has been conceptualized as encompassing the central, enduring, and distinctive attributes of an organization.

How we act in specific situations is reciprocally related to one's identity, the roles that we have identified as important, and the congruence between our behavior and how we believe we ideally should behave.

Social identity is correlated with individual identity and deals with one's perceived role as a member of a group as opposed to one's identity as a unique individual identity at the personal level. This is validated by comparing the self to others and by confirming one's identity in context with how one believes one is perceived by others.

The process of self-assessment in evaluating our behavior is complex, typically occurring at the unconscious and sub-conscious levels that we use to control our behavior to comply with whom we believe we are. In the self-assessment process, we compare ourselves to others who are both like us and different from us in determining our self-image and identities. Our social and personal identities may integrate both our self-perceptions and the attributes that make up those identities.

Whereas identity explains who we believe we are, self-awareness includes the degree to which we are sensitive to how we are perceived by others. Self-awareness research suggests people who have greater self-awareness about how they are perceived by others are better at integrating that information into their self-appraisals, and, by extension, into their behavior.

Applying identity and self-awareness to leadership effectiveness, a leader's awareness of how subordinates perceive the leader has important consequences. Leaders are able to become more effective when they demonstrate that they are receptive to feedback from others.

Values

What are the principles or values that you live your life by? What do you stand for? What are you willing to sacrifice or even die for? The answer to those questions can be defined by our values.

Values are the principles and standards that motivate us in life. They are our basic conviction that tells us what is right, good or worthy. Values are like an internal compass. Value congruence is the extent to which an individual's behavior is consistent with the stated value. Examples of values include honesty, integrity, friendship, family, challenge, harmony, compassion or loyalty.

Great leaders are crystal clear about what they value and how their values guide their behavior and decisions.

Clarifying your values involves two steps: Becoming clear about your most important values and communicating those values to others through your words and actions.

INSEAD Advanced Management Program professors Ian C. Woodward and Sanah Shaffakat developed an integrated model of a personal values system called Understanding Values for Insightfully Aware Leaders. In their study of 163 owners, senior and middle managers, they found that executives' values had a direct and significant impact on organizational performance, whereas age, tenure, experience and education did not. Other studies show that values impact employee satisfaction, commitment, productivity and performance.

When values are understood and communicated, many more transparent conversations can occur between leaders and workers. Values are central to authentic leadership, where leaders are deeply aware of how their values impact the lives of others. Numerous assessments exist that leaders can use to identify their most important values. Our case study, Daniel, completed a values clarification assessment and encouraged his team to do the same. Upon completion, they shared their values assessment results with each other.

Values identification and clarification can have a positive impact on a leaders' self-awareness by being able to reflect upon what's most important to them, and using that insight to inform them regarding subsequent decisions, actions and relationships.

5

What Does Self-Awareness Research Tell Us?

"Without deep reflection one knows from daily life that one exists for other people."

Albert Einstein

Self-awareness has been a fundamental issue in literature, philosophy and psychology as a basis for studying human behavior and motivation.

In recent years, research on self-awareness as it applies to leaders has been rejuvenated, partly because of considerable evidence that bad leaders lack self-awareness and this often leads to failure.

Part of the research on self-awareness has involved looking at how the brain plays a role. Neuroscientist V.S. Ramachandran has speculated that mirror neurons may provide the neurological basis of human self-awareness, arguing "these neurons can not only help simulate other people's behavior but can be turned 'inward--as it were--to create second-order representations or metarepresentations of your own earlier brain processes."

25

In their influential book *A Theory of Objective Self-Awareness*, Shelley Duval and Robert Wicklund contend when we focus our attention on ourselves, we evaluate and compare our current behavior to our internal standards and values, eliciting a state of objective self-awareness, becoming self-conscious as objective evaluators of ourselves.

Our belief in our ability to succeed, often referred to as "self-efficacy," sets the stage to how we think, behave and feel. People with strong self-efficacy are aware of their flaws and abilities and choose to utilize these qualities to the best of their ability. People who lack self-efficacy can evade challenges and quickly feel discouraged by setbacks partly because they are not self-aware, and therefore do not always change their attitude.

Internal Awareness of Self

Cognitive scientist Lars Hall argues that introspection, a particular kind of internal self-reflection, can raise self-awareness. It is the skill and practice of examining the characters, traits, beliefs, values, strengths, abilities, motivations and desires that form a person's identity and make an accurate assessment of them. In other words, it is an understanding of how we think and feel in different situations about different aspects of self. This awareness shapes a person's decisions and determines his/her actions and behaviors.

Psychologist Daryl J. Bem of Cornell University says people learn about themselves by passively examining their own behavior rather than understanding the thoughts and feelings to derive conclusions about self. This can act as a compass for decision-making and modification of individual behavior.

There were many instances in coaching leaders when they were facing difficult decisions or situations when I would ask them "what is the emotion you are feeling right now?" and all too often the response was "I don't know," or I would get a reply that described their thoughts, not their emotions.

A critical component of internal emotional self-awareness is the practice of noticing and labelling your emotions when they happen. The noticing and labelling practices assist in gaining clarity as to "what is" in the present moment. It helps us to gain some insight into our relationship with ourselves, with our experiences, with others and with our environment. Usually when we have "a thought," we engage with it automatically, fusing with it. As we know, some thoughts can be very sticky, making it difficult to step back. With mindfulness, we practice gently pulling away from thoughts, again and again, pausing, observing, creating more and more space between the "mental event" and the response.

Each time, at the moment, when we are practicing noting and labelling, we are re-wiring the brain, because we are doing something different than what we would normally do. Each time we are noting and labelling, we are disengaging from the default mode network. Instead of automatically engaging with the thought, we are stepping out of thought, creating a space; allowing for choosing and responding rather than reacting, and becoming the wise observer of our mind. In this way, we are less at the mercy of our default mode, which can get stuck in unhelpful rumination and preoccupation. When we become more aware, we wake up and free ourselves from our conditioning, and we begin to live in a more conscious and intentional way.

Research in neuroscience has shown that the labelling of thought helps to regulate emotion and promote insight during times of stress and emotional upset. Labelling with kindness is very beneficial as it slows the thinking mind, creating a space in our mind, where we can step back and observe. This has the effect also of calming the stress reaction in our body and not getting caught in the intensity of the emotion.

Research has shown that mental noticing and labelling help us to improve the emotional wiring in our brains. It produces a relaxing effect in our body, which helps us detach from thoughts. We stop identifying so personally with our thoughts and reacting emotionally to them. Rather than getting caught up in our thoughts, we train our minds to notice and label. Then we have more choice in terms of which thoughts we can intentionally pay attention to. By de-emphasizing the rumination or emotion with our attention, through noting and labelling, we can free ourselves from excessive preoccupation or reactivity, becoming calmer, being abler to turn to the good things in our lives.

In the case study of Robert that I described earlier, often he was unaware of the emotions that he was feeling at the time he was feeling them, and when asked to describe or label them at the moment, he was frequently unable to do so. This was particularly evident during situations in which his stress level was elevated. Thus, being unaware of his internal state, his responses to others and events were often reactive, sometimes with seriously negative results.

In contrast, the other case study in the book, Daniel, had deliberately adopted the combination mindfulness-cognitive awareness practice of tuning into his physical state, and being able to label and describe for himself his emotional state while he was engaging in actions or words.

The Social or External Side of Self-Awareness: How Others Perceive Us

Self-awareness is not only an internal phenomenon but a social or external phenomenon too. We get the reflection of ourselves through the human mirrors, that is, from others' opinions, responses and reactions.

Self-aware people have the ability to see how others view them and understand the impact of their behavior on others.

Even skilled leaders who recognize the importance of tuning into the nuances of interpersonal relationships fall prey to the compelling problems, uncertainty, and often uncontrollable situations that highjack their physiological responses, exponentially increase stress, and cause inevitable self-awareness dysfunction.

Richard Boyatzis and Annie McKee, co-authors with Daniel Goleman of the book *Primal Leadership,* have noted that under times of stress, individuals become less self-aware and miss the signs from others that enable them to be effective in managing themselves and their relationships.

In Robert's case again, in interactions with his team and colleagues, he could be oblivious to their emotional or mental states, because either he failed to notice body language signals or failed to elicit verbal feedback from them regarding his actions or words. As a result, his perception of the reality of the situation was vastly different than others in the same situation.

In contrast, the other case study, Daniel, had developed the practices of noticing the body language of others while he spoke or acted, and also eliciting feedback (both formal and informal) on an ongoing basis, so that his perception of reality was either similar or very different than that from others. This in turn would inform him about what to do next.

6

Why is it So Difficult to be Self-Aware?

"Your visions will become clear only when you can look into your own heart. Who looks outside, dreams; who looks inside, awakes."

C.G. Jung

If self-awareness is so important, why do so many people have difficulty with it? Part of the answer to that question, other than a person's unwillingness, is the influence of self-deception, "blind spots" and biases.

Self-awareness avoidance may take many forms, including watching TV, engaging in social media, escaping into alcohol, drugs or other addictions, or even committing suicide.

Defense Mechanisms

Researchers Cam Caldwell and Linda Hayes explain how defense mechanisms such as projection, displacement, undoing, isolation, sublimation, and denial are virtually universal phenomena and can lead to feedback-avoiding behavior. Other researchers suggest that anticipating a desired conclusion and viewing the world through a self-serving bias can directly affect the way in which people gather evidence and reach conclusions about themselves.

Self-Deception

The problem of congruence in how we assess ourselves is essential to self-awareness, one's individual identity, and the degree of self-deception. As a form of cognitive dissonance, self-deception has been described as a discrepancy between the way in which we know how we ought to act and how we actually behave. Self-deception is one of many defense mechanisms that enable us to maintain self-esteem and our identity.

The tendency to believe in faulty preconceptions is consistent with several types of self-deception identified by University of Washington psychologist, Frederick A. Ziegler, as eight rationalizations that frequently occur. Those eight perceptions and their respective meanings are:

- **A pretense to others.** Claiming prior knowledge about the likelihood of an uncertain outcome may be either a rationalization or an attempt to look good in others' eyes.
- **Discount of a failure.** Claiming to have known in advance that failure was likely may be an attempt to persuade oneself that one truly knew about an uncertain probability.
- **Articulation of past fears.** Unwillingness to deal with uncertainty may result in claiming foreknowledge of a likely failure – but after that disappointment actually occurs.
- **Inability to understand.** Although evidence of a fact contrary to what we may want to believe may be present, our failure to acknowledge a situation may legitimately reflect something we cannot emotionally deal with or understand.
- **Wanting reality to be different.** One's biases affect how we

see the world and affect the formation of our beliefs so powerfully that we get dissuaded by wishful thinking.

- **Intentional averting of attention.** We know intuitively that something is unbearably distressing and deliberately avoid addressing a painful issue so that we do not have to deal with it.
- **Resolving to change.** At times, we acknowledge that we have not dealt with issues that we ought to have addressed in the past.
- **Acknowledging regret.** We may express the fact that we should have been attuned to key information in the past, but overlooked key clues.

Understanding how we deceive ourselves can enable us to avoid those tendencies that erode relationships with others and that lower our self-esteem. In writing about self-deception as a coping mechanism, Daniel Goleman explained that self-deception was often a sub-conscious effort to avoid pain and anxiety, skewing our conscious awareness by filtering out painful information. Psychiatrist Scott Peck, author of *The Road Less Travelled*, noted that frequently those who deceive others or themselves do so unwittingly and often without a conscious awareness of their motives for their deceptions.

In writing about the dissonance of self-deception, Richard Boyatzis and Annie McKee describe it as follows: "We end up seeing the world in very black-and-white terms, and we slowly lose the ability to see ourselves, or those around us, realistically.

We miss a lot. Then, when things do go wrong, it is very easy to continue to blame others, and feel sorry for ourselves as things deteriorate--especially when the downturn feels like a surprise and follows a period of denial."

Another reason we can deceive ourselves about reality and are not aware, is because we are "not present" a good part of the time, but rather, our minds are in the past or the future. Another way is saying this is that a person is not mindful.

Psychologists Matthew Killingworth and Daniel T. Gilbert found, in their research, almost half of the time our minds wander to somewhere or something else other than here and now, noting that our brain's tendency--particularly as we get older--operates on an unconscious "automatic pilot."

Blind Spots

In the book by Ann E. Tenbrunsel and Max H. Bazerman *Blind Spots: Why We Fail to Do What's Right and What to Do About It,* they argue good people do bad things without knowing that they are doing anything wrong. This can also create motivational blindness, which is the tendency to not notice the unethical actions of others when it is against our own best interests to notice. Blind spots also create the "want" self--that part of us that behaves according to self-interest and, often, without regard for moral principles.

Robert Bruce Shaw, in his book, *Leadership Blindspots: How Successful Leaders Identify and Overcome the Weaknesses That Matter,* describes the 20 most common blind spots he has seen while working as an executive coach for hundreds of professionals. Shaw describes how blind spots hinder leaders from being effective by:

Overestimating their strategic capabilities. Shaw says this is often the blind spot of leaders who have strong operational experience, but then get promoted to higher more strategic, visionary positions.

Valuing being right over being effective. This blind spot, Shaw argues, occurs when a leader thinks he or she has all the answers, and is unwilling to listen to others' viewpoints.

In addition to experience, executives' positional power can hinder their self-awareness. Studies have shown that people don't always learn the right lessons from experience. Expertise doesn't always guarantee seeing the right information or making the right decisions. Overconfidence can often be the result. Business professor James O'Toole has observed that, as one's positional power grows, one's willingness to listen to others shrinks.

Biases

A cognitive bias is a systematic pattern of deviation from the norm or rationality in judgment. Individuals create their own "subjective social reality" from their perceptions, which then may dictate their behavior in the social world. As a result, cognitive biases may lead to perceptual distortions, inaccurate judgment, illogical interpretation, or what we know as a lack of rational thinking.

Not all biases are conscious. Unconscious bias is a survival mechanism that helps our brains sift through large amounts of sensory information and influences our perceptions of people and situations, and how we behave in response.

A study by James S. Jones and his colleagues found that biases often develop outside of our control. As we learn more about bias, psychologists have come to believe biases are a hard-wired aspect of our brain and our behavior. They contend our ancient minds know that survival can be dependent on snap decisions, so biases help us make these decisions quickly--often without us being conscious. We have so much information coming at us, it's much easier for our minds to continue to follow what's familiar and expected versus what's not--hence, why "change" can be such a stressful event in our lives.

Unconscious cognitive biases can have a significant negative effect on our self-awareness, particularly our social self-awareness. As we become unaware, blind or reject how other people see us, we make decisions based upon those biases, which may distort reality.

Our case study Robert suffered both from blind spots and biases. First, his major blind spot was a belief that he had all the answers and was always right, even in the face of evidence to prove otherwise. He was blind to the reality that others may have valid and accurate perspectives, and that he might, on occasion, be wrong. His major bias was a confirmation bias, in that he always looked for information to validate his beliefs and ignore information that was contrary.

In contrast, Daniel had engaged with his coach to identify what might potentially be blind spots and biases and incorporated that information into his effort to both be willing to admit he didn't have the answers or could be wrong, and take steps to validate the perspectives of others even if they didn't agree with his.

Self-Assessment Inaccuracies

A common approach to raising self-awareness is self-reporting assessments, which are more prevalent than 360 degree assessments which involve the assessment by others. Recent research shows that there is questionable accuracy for self-assessments.

In one study of more than 13,000 professionals, researchers found almost no relationships between self-assessment and objective performance ratings. A second study by these researchers found more than 33% of engineers rated their performance in the top 5% relative to peers.

Another study showed that 94% of college professors thought they were above average in their jobs. In 2001, 91% of Harvard University students graduated with honors, and in 2013, 50% of all grades awarded were A's. By 2015, 72% of students didn't think grade inflation was a problem.

Yet, the reliability of self-assessments and lack of self-awareness is significant. One study showed that employees who lacked self-awareness reduced decision quality by 36% and increased conflict by 30%. Another study with hundreds of publically traded companies found that those with poor financial returns were 79% more likely to employ large numbers of employees who were not self-aware.

Accurately Assessing Self-Awareness

There are numerous ways in which leaders can become more self-aware. Here's a partial list. Many on this list can be described as self-assessments, which are extremely valuable. However, to develop social or external self-awareness (i.e., how others see you), obtaining feedback either through a formal assessment or informal conversation is even more valuable.

1. **Emotional Intelligence assessments.** A good example is the EQi Assessment (with a 360 component) which has been used as a powerful coaching tool.

2. **Strengths assessment.** The Values in Action Strength Test from the University of Pennsylvania will highlight your most natural strengths and your weaknesses.

3. **The Self-Awareness Outcomes Questionnaire.** The SAOQ is an attempt to capture the range of effects that self-awareness has on an individual's everyday life.

4. **The Reflection/Rumination Questionnaire** measures the extent to which a person tends to think about or reflect on self.

5. **The Mindful Attention Awareness Scale** which measures mindfulness traits.

6. **The Self-Reflection and Insight Scale** which measures the tendency to reflect on the self and the extent to which individuals have insight into their own behavior.

7. **Taking self-reflection time.** Take time each evening to reflect on your behavior for the day. How do you perceive yourself? How do others perceive you? What can you learn from observing your behavior today?

8. **Personal values assessment.** Identifying core values which answer the question: what's most important to me? When you become aware of your personal values, you can evaluate if you're living in accord with them.

9. **Developing your personal vision, purpose and mission statements.** You have an ideal future self. This future self is your realized innate potential. Being able to also identify and clarify your life purpose and mission which go far beyond describing them as your job, helps raise self-awareness.

10. **Journaling.** Capturing your inner thoughts and feelings in a journal helps you objectify them.

11. **Writing your life story.** Your life story is a fundamental component of your personality. Psychologist Dan

McAdams says, "The stories we tell ourselves about our lives don't just shape our personalities—they are our personalities."

12. **Shadow work.** We are complex creatures with opposing tensions within us. For every aspect of our character we identify with, an opposing quality lives within our unconscious. Shadow work seeks to bring these opposing qualities to light so they won't influence our behavior.

13. **Reflecting on your "Inner Dialogue."** Within our minds is a family of inner voices (or sub personalities) with their thoughts, feelings, and behaviors. Dialoguing with these characters out loud or in a journal helps us develop self-awareness of our emotional terrain.

14. **Mindfulness meditation.** During mindfulness meditation, you can develop the practice and skill of reflecting both on your inner state (thoughts and emotions), as well as your external state through observation and noticing without judgment.

15. **A 360-degree feedback assessment.** This is a process through which feedback from an employee's subordinates, colleagues, and supervisors is gathered and compared to your own self-assessment. Such feedback can also include, when relevant, feedback from external sources who interact with the employee, such as customers and suppliers or other interested stakeholders.

The Appendices in this book contain some examples that may be useful for you.

I Know Myself and Neither Do You

7

How "Busyness" Interferes with Self-Awareness

"The greatest enemy of good thinking is busyness."

John C. Maxwell

Modern lives have contributed to our inability to engage in self-reflection and raise our self-awareness, because we rarely find time to do so--or at least that's become an excuse.

"If you live in America in the 21st century, you've probably had to listen to many people tell you how busy they are. It's become the default response when you ask anyone how they're doing," contends Tin Kreider, in his article, "The Busy Trap," in the *New York Times*. He says often they say this as a boast, "disguised as a complaint," but often these same people complain about being dead tired and exhausted.

We can define busyness as a state of having a lot of activity, or of not being idle. You can be overloaded, overwhelmed, snowed, swamped, tied up and stressed. You feel like there is not enough time for all the activities you are committed to or want to do.

We live in a culture obsessed with being busy: "Western society puts a high value on being busy," wrote Dr. Christiane Northup, a women's health expert and *New York Times* best-selling author. "We are conditioned to believe that being busy equates to being good, worthy, and successful."

In his article for *Harvard Business Review,* renowned business leader and author Greg McKeown calls it "The More Bubble," and argues society has granted us permission to be proud of being busy. "This bubble is being enabled by an unholy alliance between three powerful trends: smart phones, social media, and extreme consumerism," he explained. "The result is not just information overload, but opinion overload. We are more aware than at any time in history of what everyone else is doing and, therefore, what we 'should' be doing." In the process, McKeown says, "we have been sold a bill of goods: that success means being supermen and superwomen who can get it all done. Of course, we back-door-brag about being busy: It's code for being successful and important."

Where does the "supermen and superwomen" imperative come from? In the business world, it often comes from the cultural expectations of high achievement. As McKeown explains, it also comes from the impression we get that everyone is doing tons of cool stuff all the time. It's an interesting take: Is our "addiction" to chaos and busyness driven more by habit and boredom--even shame?

Whatever it is, the busy "humblebrag" is just a coping mechanism. "Most of us aren't genuinely proud of our chaotic lives … we just hide behind the reverence every time we fail to break the cycle," McKeown says, "And while being ambitious (to some degree) is obviously a great thing, it's important that we don't allow these cultural expectations to push us to the point of burnout."

U.S.A. Today published a multi-year poll in 2008, to determine how people perceived time and their own busyness. It found that in each consecutive year since 1987, people reported that they were busier than the year before, with 69% responding that they were either "busy," or "very busy," with only 8% responding that they were "not very busy." Not surprisingly, women reported being busier than men, and those between ages 30 to 60 were the busiest. When the respondents were asked what they were sacrificing to their busyness, 56% cited sleep, 52% recreation, 51% hobbies, 44% friends and 30% family. In 1987, 50% said they ate at least one family meal everyday; by 2008, that figure had declined to 20%.

A Harvard Business School survey of 1,000 professionals found that 94% worked at least 50 hours a week, and almost half worked over 65 hours. Other research shows that the share of college-educated American men regularly working over 50 hours a week rose from 24% in 1979 to 28% in 2006. According to another survey, 60% of those who use smartphones are connected to work for 13.5 hours or more a day. European labor laws rein in overwork; in the U.S. 40% of managers say they put in over 60 hours a week.

Dr. Susan Koven practices internal medicine at Massachusetts General Hospital. In a 2013 *Boston Globe* column, she wrote: "In the past few years, I've observed an epidemic of sorts: Patient after patient suffering from the same condition. The symptoms of this condition include fatigue, irritability, insomnia, anxiety, headaches, heartburn, bowel disturbances, back pain, and weight gain. There are no blood tests or X-rays diagnostic of this condition, and yet it's easy to recognize. The condition is excessive busyness."

Brigid Schulte, in her 2014 book, *Overwhelmed,* writes incisively about this trend, "So much do we value busyness, researchers have found a human 'aversion' to idleness and need for 'justifiable busyness.'"

Busyness, Multitasking and Productivity

"Nowadays we're expected to accomplish much more with our time," says David Levy, Ph.D., professor at the School of Information at the University of Washington. In an attempt to get extra work done, we "multitask, always trying to do two or three things at the same time. So we may eat our fast-food lunch and conduct business calls while we're driving or checking our email. Rarely do we focus our attention on just one task anymore." A big negative to all this multitasking, he adds, is that it is far more intellectually draining than single tasking.

David Meyer from the University of Michigan published a study that showed that switching what you're doing mid-task increases the time it takes you to finish both tasks by 25%. "Multitasking is going to slow you down, increasing the chances of mistakes," Meyer said. "Disruptions and interruptions are a bad deal from the standpoint of our ability to process information."

Microsoft studied this phenomenon in their workers and found that it took people an average of 15 minutes to return to their important projects (such as writing reports or computer code) every time they were interrupted by emails, phone calls or other messages. They didn't spend the 15 minutes on the interrupting messages, either; the interruptions led them to stray to other activities, such as surfing the Internet for pleasure.

When you try to do two things at once, researchers have concluded that your brain can't perform both tasks successfully. René Marois and his colleagues at Vanderbilt University argued "We are under the impression that we have this brain that can do more than it can. We're so enamored with multitasking that we think we're getting more done, even though our brains aren't physically capable of this. Regardless of what we might think, we are most productive when we manage our schedules enough to ensure that we can focus effectively on the task at hand. That implies doing less, not doing more."

There are other factors at play. Mobile devices can reach employees anywhere, anytime. "We can't get away from work anymore," says Gabe Ignatow, Ph.D., a sociologist at the University of North Texas who studies social change. "Even when we're relaxing on the weekends, we're often bombarded with emails, text messages and calls from the office."

Other digital distractions--namely, social media--can make us feel even more inundated. "Many people feel like they have to keep up with the endless stream of Facebook, Twitter and other social media posts, so that consumes even more of our time," Ignatow adds.

In essence, we have lost our belief in *Dolce Far Niente*," or how sweet to do nothing." Our inability to do this is exacerbated by our incapacity to unplug from the digital world. I argued in my article "Why it's so hard to unplug from the digital world," in Medium.com, that we may be actually addicted to the digital virtual world, which can physically disconnect us from others and our inner selves.

45

In my article in *Psychology Today*, "Workaholism and the myth of hard work," I argued that a "contributing factor to the problem of workaholism is the prevailing belief in hard work as the route to success, particularly wealth. Notions of hard work are predominantly held by the middle class and poor people and originate from the industrial revolution and Protestant religious tenants, which viewed hard work both as a virtue and magic formula for success. Hard work has never been a belief embraced by the upper class and wealthy."

A Business Roundtable study found that after just eight 60-hour weeks the fall-off in productivity is so marked that the average team would have accomplished as much if they had kept to a 40-hour work week. And 70-or 80-hour weeks, the fall-off happens even faster; at 80 hours, the break-even point is reached in just three weeks. Studies on this subject conducted by the Bureau of Labor Statistics, U.S. Department of Labor, Proctor and Gamble Company, the National Electrical Contractors Association, and the Mechanical Contractors Association of American produced similar results. All of them showed that continuing scheduled overtime has a strong negative effect on productivity, which increases in magnitude proportionate to the amount and duration of overtime.

Critics of these studies cite the fact that they focus on physical jobs and don't apply to the majority of employees who are "knowledge workers." Robinson argues that research shows that knowledge workers have fewer productive working hours in a day than physical worker--about six. U.S. military research has shown that losing just one hour of sleep per night for a week will cause a level of cognitive degradation equivalent to a .10 blood alcohol level. And what's worse, most of them "typically have no idea of just how impaired they are," says Robinson. Robinson cites the follow-up investigations on the Exxon Valdez disaster and the Challenger explosion, where investigators determined that overworked, overtired decision-makers played a significant role in those disasters.

How Our Beliefs About Busyness Hinder Self-Awareness

If you're reading this on your phone or tablet, and rushing to work while hunting for your headphones, then you need to stop. At least, that's what Søren Kierkegaard, the Danish philosopher who lived at the beginning of the 19th century, might advise. And indeed, as we race from the office to the gym to a dinner, proudly showing off our jam-packed schedules, it's worth remembering Kierkegaard's warnings about busyness long ago. He wrote: "Of all ridiculous things the most ridiculous seems to me, to be busy—to be a man who is brisk about his food and his work...What, I wonder, do these busy folks get done?"

Stephen Evans, a philosophy professor at Baylor University, explains that Kierkegaard saw busyness as a means of distracting oneself from truly important questions, such as who you are and what life is for. Busy people "fill up their time, always find things to do," but they have no principle guiding their life. "Everything is important but nothing is important," he adds.

Without answering crucial and terrifying questions about life, without deciding on a unified purpose, Kierkegaard believed that one could not develop a self. He called those without one unified purpose "double minded," and argued that this mindset causes busyness. And so busyness and lack of self are a bit of a chicken-and-egg situation. "If you don't have a self, you don't want to be aware of that," Evans says. "You always have to stay busy."

Kierkegaard's concerns about busyness are also connected with his view of time, and the importance of living in the present. "The unhappy man is always absent from himself, never present to himself," he wrote. In other words, obsessing over future goals, and keeping frenetically busy with an eye to some far-off date, is a way of distracting oneself from present reality.

And while Kierkegaard didn't directly address the issue of busyness and its negative impact on self-awareness, the connection to me is obvious. If you're too busy doing things, how can you take the time to reflect on what you are doing, both internally and externally?

Being busy is not a virtue, and it's not a badge of honor. We are human beings, not human doings.

8

How Self-Esteem Has Damaged Self-Awareness

"We do not serve the healthy development of young people when we convey that self-esteem may be achieved by reciting 'I am special' every day, or by stroking one's own face while saying 'I love me.'"

Nathaniel Branden, *The Six Pillars of Self-Esteem*

Accurate self-awareness and self-assessment become far more difficult if we have a distorted or exaggerated view of ourselves. Some experts blame the self-esteem movement of the last few decades for this development.

Self-esteem can be defined as an individual's subjective evaluation of their own worth. Social psychologists and co-authors of *Social Psychology (4th Edition)*, Eliot Smith and Diane Mackie have defined it: "The self-concept is what we think about the self; self-esteem, is the positive or negative evaluations of the self, as in how we feel about it."

The American psychologist Albert Ellis criticized on numerous occasions the concept of self-esteem as essentially self-defeating and ultimately destructive. Although acknowledging the human propensity and tendency to ego rating as innate, he has critiqued the philosophy of self-esteem as unrealistic, illogical and destructive -- often doing more harm than good.

These days, self-esteem has acquired a second meaning: "an unduly high opinion of oneself; vanity." It is this definition that best fits Generation Y, according to Jean M. Twenge, professor of psychology at San Diego State University. She argues inflated egos leave many young people with unrealistic expectations, and their inability to achieve these can lead to depression. It is no coincidence, she says, that the U.S. Center for Disease Control and Prevention in Atlanta, Georgia, reported that one in nine Americans over the age of 12 now takes antidepressants --a quadrupling of the rate since the late 1980s.

Twenge sees another sign of dangerously overblown self-esteem in rising levels of narcissism. She found that twice as many college students had high levels of narcissism in 2006 compared with the early 1980s. Narcissists tend to be intolerant of criticism and prone to cheating and aggression. "These are the people who wind up in your office arguing over a grade," she says. In her latest book, *The Narcissism Epidemic,* written with co-author W. Keith Campbell, she recounts anecdotes of people hiring fake paparazzi to make themselves look famous, and buying "McMansions" on credit, as evidence of the Americans' overblown ego.

"We have taken individualism too far," says Twenge, and popular culture reflects this. She has worked with University of Kentucky social psychologist Nathan DeWall and others to chart an increase in the frequency of the word "I" in the lyrics of hit U.S. pop songs from 1980 to 2007.

Twenge blames four factors: Changes in parenting styles, the cult of celebrity, the internet and easy credit. "All of these things allow people to have an inflated sense of self in which the appearance of performance is more important than the actual performance," she says.

Tasha Eurich argues persuasively that we are "living in an age of focus on self and self- aggrandizement." This corresponds to the rise of the age of self-esteem. Eurich goes on to say "an excessive self–focus obscures our vision of those around us and distorts our ability to see ourselves as we really are." She quotes the research that shows an inverse relationship between how special we think we are and how self-aware we are.

Psychologist Roy Baumeister has studied the issue of self-esteem extensively. He reviewed 15,000 studies and found:

- The relationship between self-esteem and success was virtually non existent.
- People with high self-esteem are more violent and aggressive, and more likely to have relationship problems.

How Narcissism Negates Self-Awareness in Leaders

In its extreme form, exaggerated self-esteem in leaders can show up as narcissism. And narcissistic leaders in North America have been very successful from a financial perspective.

A research study completed by Charles A. O'Reilly III at Stanford's business school surveyed employees in 32 large, publicly traded tech companies. He contends that bosses who exhibit narcissistic traits like dominance, self-confidence, a sense of entitlement, grandiosity and low empathy, tend to make more money than their less self-centered counterparts, even if the lower-paid CEOs exhibit plenty of confidence. O'Reilly says of the narcissists, "they don't really care what other people think and depending on the nature of the narcissist, they are impulsive and manipulative." O'Reilly goes on to argue the longer narcissistic leaders are at the helm, the higher their compensation in comparison with the rest of the leadership team, or in some cases the narcissistic bosses fire anyone who dares to question or challenge them.

There is a dark downside to this appearance of success, however, O'Reilly contends. Company morale often declines, and employees leave the company. And while the narcissistic or abusive leaders may bring in the bigger pay checks, O'Reilly says there is compelling evidence that they don't perform any better than lower-paid, less narcissistic counterparts. This argument has been supported by Michael Maccoby in his book, *The Productive Narcissist: The Promise and Peril of Visionary Leadership.*

Maccoby points out that tech firms, particularly those in Silicon Valley, are where abusive leaders thrive. His article on the subject in the *Harvard Business Review* received an overwhelming response of affirmation. He says in business and sports it is assumed if you are a big winner, you can get away with being a jerk. Stanford University professor Robert Sutton argues such bosses and cultures drive good people out and claims bad bosses affect the bottom line through increased turnover, absenteeism, decreased commitment and performance. He says the time spent counselling or appeasing these people, consoling victimized employees, reorganizing departments or teams and arranging transfers produce significant hidden costs for the company. And he warns organizations that narcissistic behavior is contagious.

INSEAD business school Professors Gianpiero Petriglieri and Jennifer Petriglieri, authors of "Can Business Schools Humanize Leadership?" argue that we have experienced a "dehumanization of leadership" in which leadership is reduced from a cultural enterprise to a strict intellectual or commercial one, and in which leadership "distances aspiring leaders from their followers and institutions, resulting in a disconnect their inner and outer worlds."

In my article "Why Do We Idolize the Narcissistic Boss, When We Know the Humble Ones Produce Better Results," in *The Financial Post*, I argue "We all tend to be hypocritical about what makes a good leader--even management experts. We exalt and praise leaders who are nasty and abusive because they are financially successful; meanwhile, research shows that humble leaders whose focus is to serve others, are equally successful, and capture the hearts and loyalty of others."

It's my estimate that approximately 30% of the leaders I have coached over the past three decades displayed clear signs of narcissism. And in virtually all of these instances, the leaders lacked self-awareness. Robert, our case study in this book, exhibited clear signs of narcissism, thinking that others existed to serve his needs, and acting in an aggressive manner when he didn't get his way.

I Know Myself and Neither Do You

9

How Mindless Work Diminishes Self-Awareness

"Not only do we as individuals get locked into single-minded views, but we also reinforce these views for each other until the culture itself suffers the same mindlessness."

Ellen Langer

Mindlessness is not the same as ignorance. Rather, mindlessness is a state of mind that is characterized by reliance on past memories. When people are mindless, they are trapped in a rigid perspective, insensitive to the ways in which reality has changed. The past dominates, and they behave much like unconscious automatons, where rules and routines govern rather than guide what they do. Essentially, the cognitive functions "freeze" and they become oblivious to subtle changes that would have led them to act differently. And they remain unaware of the changes around them. Mindlessness is pervasive in our society and in organizations and takes its toll. Often, some people can see mindlessness in other people, but they are blind to it in themselves.

Living automatically can place us at a risk of mindlessly reacting to situations or people without reflecting on an intentional response.

For many people, living on "automatic" or essentially being mindless, is a way of life. When automatic thinking dominates our lives, we can feel numb and empty and life can become dull and repetitive.

The Mindless Organization

Mindlessness at work has become a comedy or parody in literature, media and the movies. In the TV series "The Office," Steve Carrell, playing the role of Michael Scott as Regional Manager of a Dunder-Mifflin branch in Scranton, Pennsylvania, epitomizes mindless behavior, which is characterized by a reliance on old, often outdated, and often dysfunctional behaviors and a reduced awareness of the world around him.

The movie "Office Space" highlights a mindless business culture. The movie character Milton exemplifies a mindless bureaucrat, who can only function in a culture that values mindless behavior. The story highlights how a culture of mindlessness can lead employees to unhappiness and active disengagement. A lack of employee engagement is not only evidenced by declining productivity, but also by disengagement when employees start to sabotage the firm's operations. Peter and two of his co-workers in the film take revenge by developing a plot to tweak the payment system so that small sums of customer payments will be transferred to their account.

Mindless people can be characterized as "robots." Their behavior, thoughts, and emotions are determined by routines based on things learned in the past. Some researchers argue that mindlessness is a consequence of the tendency to apply previously formed mindsets to current situations. The result: Individuals are locked into a repetitive and often unconscious approach to daily life.

The Power of Distractions and Mind Wandering

When we are immersed in media (TV and social media), we are triggering a brain chemical dopamine which creates a "high." We are hard-wired to do what it takes to maintain this elevated state. When the dopamine levels decrease, we begin to look for activities that will restore the high.

In addition, our minds naturally wander. We think or replay the past and worry about what will happen in the future. A study of 2,250 adults by two Harvard University psychologists found that peoples' minds wander an astounding 47% of the time. They concluded that a "human mind is a wandering mind, and a wandering mind is an unhappy mind."

Wandering minds can negatively affect the quality of peoples' work. "High quality attention is the productive basis for knowledge workers and we do very little to cultivate that essential resource," says Jeremy Hunter, a professor at the Peter F. Drucker School of Management in Los Angeles.

Mindless workers can be disconnected from their inner world and can escape to work as a haven. They can be on automatic pilot, allowing work to engulf them without being aware that it is. They can get an adrenaline rush from meeting impossible deadlines; and finally they are preoccupied with work even if they are not there.

Teresa Amabie and her colleagues at Harvard Business School evaluated the daily work patterns of more than 9,000 individuals working on projects that required creativity and innovation. They found that the likelihood of creative thinking is higher when people focus on one activity for a significant part of the day and collaborate with only one person. Conversely, when people had fragmented days with many activities and meetings and discussions with lots of people, their creative thinking declined significantly.

The calendars of CEOs and senior executives are often booked back to back all day based on the proposition that it is both necessary and leads to greater productivity, despite the evidence that it doesn't. CEOs have to learn how to delegate most matters to subordinates, and return contacts from others when convenient. They need to edit or shut off the flow of incoming information and completely unplug for blocks of time, and give up the need to be on top of everything.

Recent studies into multitasking specifically show deficits in memory and learning when juggling cognitive load. Researchers at Duke University reported over 40% of our behaviors are based on habits, not conscious decisions. If unconscious habits and assumptions aren't fixed, if we aren't aware of them and act to correct them, then the force of these habits will continue to govern our behaviors and decisions.

When negative external events occur, internally the mind ruminates and anxiety and stress increase. We become hijacked by internal suffering. When we practice mindful working, we use our minds to navigate workplace woes with clarity, self-compassion, courage and creativity.

Cognitive Overload Contributes to Mindlessness and Lack of Self-Awareness in Leaders

The demands of leadership can produce "power stress," a side effect of being in a position of power and influence that often leaves even the best leaders physically and emotionally drained.

As a result, leaders can easily find themselves moving from an "approach" orientation to their work characterized by being emotionally open, engaged and innovative, to an "avoidance" orientation that is characterized by aversion, irritability, aggression, fear and close-mindedness.

If leaders believe they don't have the time to work through all aspects of a problem, they are inclined to be narrow in perspective and take cognitive shortcuts and become more impulsive and reactive. Their actions, in effect, become "mindless" and automatic.

Daniel Siegel contends that a corporate culture of cognitive shortcuts results in oversimplification, curtailed curiosity, reliance on ingrained beliefs and the development of perceptional blind spots. He argues that mindfulness practices enable individuals to jettison judgment and develop more flexible feelings toward what before may have been mental events they tried to avoid, or towards which they had intense adverse reactions.

David Rock, writing in *Psychology Today*, argues "busy people who run our companies and institutions tend to spend little time thinking about themselves and other people, but a lot of time thinking about strategy, data and systems. As a result, the circuits involved in thinking about oneself and other people, the medial prefrontal cortex, tend to be not too well developed." Rock says "speaking to an executive about mindfulness can be a bit like speaking to a classical musician about jazz."

Robert, our case study in the book, was fairly representative of many leaders in organizations with whom I observed and/or coached, in that they often worked on automatic pilot without adequate reflection of what they were doing, and were "multi-taskers." The worst of them would even interrupt themselves while speaking in order to respond to a smartphone text or notification on their computer screen. In essence they were not mindful, and rarely were self-aware.

10

The Case for Self-Reflection

"Let go of rejections and focus on self-reflection. For it is within that you will find the light you seek."

Amy Leigh Mercree

Self-reflection can be defined as "serious thought about one's character and actions"; "the activity of thinking about your own feelings and behavior, and the reasons that may lie behind them"; and "the examination or observation of one's own mental and emotional processes."

Reflective thinking is important because the world is not predictable, and new or unexpected events take place. During reflective thinking, we pause to examine the consequences of various actions and events and it helps us make decisions.

Reflective skills harness our prefrontal capacity for executive attention, prosocial behavior, empathy and self-regulation. As we reflect on our own internal states, the resonance circuitry that evolved to connect with others' minds is primed to sense the deep nature of our own intentional world.

Management expert Margaret J. Wheatley has said "without reflection, we go blindly on our way, creating more unintended consequences, and failing to achieve anything useful."

Jack Mezirow, in his book, *Fostering Critical Reflection in Adulthood: A Guide to Transformative and Emancipatory Learning*, describes critical reflection as "a type of reflection characterized by an individual's reexamination of the presuppositions that inform their own beliefs, thoughts, and actions."

Learning occurs both by doing, and also by thinking about what we do. Often we go through our day-to-day life without spending too much time thinking about our experiences. Reflection is a tool to keep your thoughts and actions running through the active part of your brain before it gets to the reactive part of your brain.

At its simplest, reflection is about careful thought. But the kind of reflection that is really valuable to leaders involves the conscious consideration and analysis of beliefs and actions for the purpose of learning. Reflection gives the brain an opportunity to pause amid the chaos, untangle and sort through observations and experiences, consider multiple possible interpretations, and create meaning.

Few companies give their employees reflection time. The focus instead is on productivity and "working harder" to meet deadlines and beat the competition. Yet, new research demonstrates the value of reflection in helping people do a better job. Francesca Gino and Gary Pisano of Harvard Business School, Giada Di Stefano of HEC Paris, and Bradley Staats of the University of North Carolina have published a study that shows that "reflecting on what you've done teaches you to do it better next time." The researchers did a series of studies which showed that reflection boosts performance. "Now more than ever we seem to be living lives where we're busy and overworked, and our research shows that if we'd take some time out for reflection, we might be better off," Gino says.

Self-reflection as a method of enhancing self-awareness can have measureable productivity benefits in organizations. The researchers demonstrated that employees who spent 15 minutes at the end of the day reflecting on their work performed 23% better after only 10 days than those who did not reflect.

Leaders should adopt a pause and reflect practice at meetings and encourage others to do the same to avoid reactive behavior. This requires a change in the habits of behavior, and examining their daily practices to allow for space, reflection and the ability to ponder.

McKinsey outlines why in the *McKinsey Quarterly* article, "Recovering from Information Overload." The article argues attention fragmentation hits CEOs and their colleagues in the C-Suite particularly hard because senior executives so badly need to synthesize information from many different sources, reflect on its implications for the organization, apply judgment, make trade-offs, and arrive at good decisions.

According to the former director of the Accenture Institute of Strategic Change and coauthor of the book, *The Attention Economy: Understanding the New Currency of Business,* Tom Davenport says, "Understanding and managing attention is now the single most important determinant of business success." We're living in an attention economy in which the ability to manage our attention and the quality of it is the key to success.

Self-reflection is something that has been written about and practiced throughout human history. Self-reflection from a philosophical perspective refers to the understanding of your mentality, beliefs, and life desires. Accordingly, all of our thoughts and sensations come with our belief that our thoughts have an effect on our beliefs. In other words, our thoughts and beliefs are directly impacted by the emotions and sensations that come with those beliefs.

Harry Kraemer, clinical professor of strategy at the Kellogg School and former CEO of multibillion-dollar healthcare company Baxter International, is adamant that leaders, and leaders-to-be, need to carve self-reflection into their daily routine. "It takes only 15 minutes, and we all have 15 minutes somewhere in the day: during a commute, during exercise, during a cup of coffee. In fact, as an added benefit, reflection can lead to finding more time for what is important," he said in an interview with the Kellogg School of Management *Insight.*

Returning to the two case studies I have cited in this book, Robert and Daniel, the contrast in the practice of self-reflection could not be more stark. Robert's daily schedule was booked solid, with meeting after meeting, phone call after phone call, with no reflection time before or after his interactions. When I encouraged him to schedule brief reflection times before and after his interactions, his response was that he reflected while he was engaged, and didn't need any further reflection time. In contrast, Daniel blocked in not only brief times for reflection before and after his interactions, but also once a week for at least an hour when he reflected on how he was feeling about things that had transpired, and what to anticipate in the coming week.

Suggestions for How Leaders Can Incorporate Self-Reflection into Their Routines

1. Pause for 5-10 minutes before every phone call, face-to-face conversation, or meeting and reflect on these questions:
    - How am I feeling about the upcoming call/conversation/meeting?
    - How do I want to feel about the upcoming call/conversation/meeting?
    - What is my intention and desired outcome for the upcoming event?
    - What am I avoiding?
    - How will I How could I be more effective?
    - How can I be more authentic?
    - How can I be more inspirational?
    - Who will I be?

2. Pause for 5-10 minutes after each event and reflect on these questions:
    - How do I feel about what happened in the event?
    - How do I want to feel about what happened in the event?
    - Did I achieve my intention/desired outcome in the event?
    - What prevented me from doing so if I didn't?
    - What options do I have if there is a similar event in the future?
    - What do I need to do to follow up?
    - How did I show up during the event?
    - Who was I being?

3. Go for a walk outside the office for 10-15 minutes to reflect. Changing your environment has a beneficial impact on thinking processes.

4. Write in a journal your thoughts and feelings before and/or after the events. Committing your thinking and feeling to paper helps you organize our intentions.
5. Once a week, set aside an hour to reflect on the week's events and how you felt and thought about them as well as reflecting on what is coming up the next week. Friday or Sunday night are good days to do this.

11

Emotional Intelligence and Self-Awareness

"Socrates's injunction 'Know thyself' speaks to the keystone of emotional intelligence: awareness of one's own feelings as they occur."

Daniel Goleman

Effective leadership involves the regulation of one's own emotions. Furthermore, it involves an understanding of and an ability to influence the positive emotions of others despite the ambiguity, setbacks, or fears that they might otherwise face. Through emotional intelligence, balance is achieved by promoting the positive emotions associated with optimism and excitement, while keeping more disruptive negative emotions such as anxiety, selfishness, fear, anger and sadness in check.

Certain areas of our brain may help us balance emotions in our decision-making process, especially in situations in which the outcomes may be uncertain or ambiguous. Recent research has also shown that regions of the brain's cortex may help us guide our actions in anticipation of emotional consequences, such as fear and despair.

Neuroscientist Matt Lieberman's research, published in *Social: Why Our Brains Are Wired to Connect,* shows that the brain has what he calls a mental, physical and emotional "braking system," located behind our left and right temples, that is activated when we label an emotion in simple words. Psychologists have observed that we prefer not to talk about our emotions, and tend to suppress them instead. However, suppressing an emotional expression can backfire, making the emotion more intense, affecting memory or creating a threat response in others. Ironically, not talking about our emotions as an intuitive "control" strategy does the opposite of what we intend, leaving us less capable of dealing with people and events. Leaders who deal with intense emotions all day need to develop emotional regulation techniques that truly keep them calm under pressure. To do that effectively, leaders would have to be keenly self-aware of their emotional state from moment-to-moment.

Other research has suggested that negative emotions are stronger than positive emotions. Dr. Rick Hanson sees it as two metaphors. Negative emotions pass through our brains and stick like "Velcro" and positive emotions pass through our brains like "Teflon."

Leaders' behaviors can "infect" others around them with specific feelings, some of which can help others perform better but some leaders' negative feelings can be debilitating and inhibit others adaptive thinking. Remember, negative feelings, even the unconscious ones, will easily overwhelm positive ones. Leaders who are able to change their internal state and regulate the external expression of feelings may find it to be one of the most powerful leadership techniques.

There is also strong evidence from fMRI studies, as well as from lesion studies in neurological patients, which suggest that patients with brain injuries in the areas associated with emotional processing are not able to distinguish their own perspective from others. Overall, there appears to be a neurological explanation for why some individuals are better at understanding the feelings, emotions, and reactions of followers.

Leaders play a crucial role in creating environments that foster threat and/or reward. In a state of threat, the significantly stronger forces of the limbic system thinking processes effectively shut down the prefrontal cortex. As a result, performance is driven by fear or anxiety, inducing the stress state (in turn releasing the stress chemical cortisol), which was earlier shown to compromise performance outcomes.

When employees work with a leader who promotes reward states, the opposite psychological and physiological effects occur. The prefrontal cortex is active and integrates positively with the limbic system. The reward chemical dopamine is released into the central nervous system in response to engagement in a challenging but supportive environment, and optimal performance can be achieved.

Emotional Self-Awareness

Daniel Goleman and colleagues in their publication, *Building Blocks of Emotional Intelligence: Emotional Self-Awareness: A Primer*, argue "Emotional self-awareness is the ability to understand your own emotions and their effects on your performance...you sense how others see you and so align your self-image with a larger reality."

Leaders can ask themselves the following questions to determine their emotional self-awareness:

- Do your feelings have a flow throughout the day, fluctuating from moment to moment?
- Do you feel physical sensations from your emotions?
- Do you experience discrete feelings or emotions or are they blended?
- Do you experience intense emotions that capture the attention of others?
- Do you pay attention to your emotions and factor them into your decisions-making?

As mentioned earlier, leaders can learn to master emotional self-awareness by learning to identify and label emotions and feelings when they happen; affirm, validate and value their feelings when they occur; and use constructive thoughts to generate positive feelings. This process is a powerful building block for emotional intelligence.

Looking at our case studies, Robert and Daniel, the contrast in levels of emotional intelligence could not have been more marked. Robert's capacity to tap into his own emotions, and be sensitive to and respond positively to the emotional states of others was severely limited.

12

Mindful Self-Awareness

"Would you like to save the world from the degradation and destruction it seems destined for? Then quietly go to work on your own self-awareness. If you want to awaken all of humanity, then awaken all of yourself. If you want to eliminate the suffering in the world, then eliminate all that is dark and negative in yourself. Truly, the greatest gift you have to give is that of your own self-transformation."

Lao Tzu

"Being aware of the fullness of our experience awakens us to the inner world of our mind and immerses us completely in our lives," Daniel J. Siegel says in his book, *The Mindful Brain.* He argues that mindful awareness harnesses the social circuitry of our brains to enable us to develop an attuned relationship with our minds. In this way, he says, "awareness of awareness is a form of reflection."

Defining Mindfulness

Definitions of mindfulness describe a psychological trait; a practice of cultivating mindfulness meditation; a mode or state of awareness; or a psychological process.

71

Another definition of mindfulness is the awareness that arises through "paying attention in a particular way: on purpose, in the present moment, and nonjudgmentally."

Descriptions of mindfulness provided by most other researchers are similar. For example, one researcher defined mindfulness as "the nonjudgmental observation of the ongoing stream of internal and external stimuli as they arise". Though some researchers focus almost exclusively on the mindfulness as it pertains to focused attention, most follow the model which proposed that mindfulness encompasses two components: the self-regulation of attention; and adoption of a reflective orientation towards our experiences.

Being able to regulate one's focused attention refers to the observation and awareness of sensations, thoughts, or feelings in the present moment. It requires both the ability to focus our attention on what is occurring, as well as the ability to intentionally switch attention from one thing to another.

An additional perspective of mindfulness involves the attitudes of curiosity, openness, and acceptance. While the notion of "acceptance" can have the connotation of passivity or resignation, in the context of mindfulness acceptance refers to our ability to be open to experiences, without resorting to either extreme of excessive preoccupation with, or suppression of, those experiences. Current views of mindfulness in clinical psychology, then, point to two primary, essential elements--awareness of one's moment-to-moment experience nonjudgmentally and with acceptance.

Psychologists A.M. Haynes and G. Feldman have highlighted that mindfulness can be seen as a strategy that stands in contrast to a strategy of avoidance of emotion on the one hand and to the strategy of emotional over engagement on the other hand. Haynes and

Feldman argue mindfulness can also be viewed as a means to develop self-knowledge and wisdom.

A Summary of Research on Mindfulness

Many studies of mindfulness (mostly on meditation) to date have reported on correlations between mindfulness and psychological and physical health. Here's an edited summary of the research:

- One study found that mindfulness was related both to a lower frequency of negative automatic thoughts and to an enhanced ability to let go of those thoughts.
- Two other studies have also demonstrated an association between mindfulness and enhanced performance on tasks assessing sustained attention and persistence.
- Other findings are consistent with the premise that systematic training in mindfulness induces changes in attention, awareness, and emotion, which can be assessed and identified at subjective, behavioral, and neurobiological levels.
- Values clarification and improved behavioral self-regulation may be two additional avenues through which mindfulness training improves psychological well-being.
- When considering aspects such as sense of responsibility, authenticity, compassion, self-acceptance and character, studies have shown that mindfulness contributes to a more coherent and healthy sense of self and identity.

Mindfulness and Self-Awareness

Xiao, Qianguo and colleagues suggested in their study, "The Mindful Self" in *Frontiers in Psychology*, that engaging in mindfulness practices is closely associated with increases in positive self-attitudes, such as non-attachment (or acceptance), compassion and equanimity. Moreover, it has been suggested that mindfulness is associated with moderating the defensive tendencies associated with lower ego-involvement. Consequently, it promotes self-knowledge and self-awareness.

In addition, mindfulness can change the mode of self-focused attention, making one fully but impartially aware and attentive to what is occurring without judgment, investment, or antipathy for what appears, which leads to clarity and accuracy in people's perceptions and judgments. Within this enhanced clarity, researchers Shauna Shapiro and her colleagues argue "the process of a repeatedly arising sense of self becomes observable to the meditator and facilitates a detachment from identification with the static sense of self, which has been termed 'decentering' or 'reperceiving'."

In all, these findings suggest that mindfulness practices moderate implicit self-concepts and perspectives on the self, and encourages positive functions of the self with a shift toward healthier profiles.

Assessing Mindfulness

There are a number of reliable useful self-awareness assessments that can be a valuable resource for leaders. Questionnaires that assess mindfulness as a general trait-like tendency to be mindful in daily life include: The Freiburg Mindfulness Meditation Inventory, the Kentucky Inventory of Mindfulness Meditation skills, the Mindful Attention Awareness Scale, the Five-Facet Mindfulness Meditation Questionnaire, the Cognitive Affective Mindfulness Meditation Scale-Revised, the Toronto Mindfulness Meditation Scale-Trait Version, the Philadelphia Mindfulness Meditation Scale and the Southampton Mindfulness Meditation Questionnaire.

Appendix D contains an assessment that shows the degree to which you are mindful.

Being Versus Doing as an Expression of Self-Awareness

Organizations typically compel members to adopt a cognitive mode that supports "Doing." Workers must plan for the future, interpret complex environments, and set goals--they are focused on getting things done, mindfully or not. Clinical psychologist at Oxford University, Mark Williams describes mindfulness as reflecting the other fundamental mode of human functioning, "Being." A reorienting toward Being, rather than Doing, may represent a strikingly different mode of thought and action than is typical in organizational functioning. Being involves attending to the present without striving, whereas Doing involves cognitive operations that support the goal-oriented behavior which is the driver for most organizational life.

Every day in everything you do, your mind switches between doing mode and being mode. Both are required for healthy living. Here's the difference between the two modes of mind:

Doing

- You are aware of how things are and how they should be.
- You set a goal to fix things.
- You try harder and harder to achieve the goal.

75

- Most of your actions happen automatically, without conscious awareness.
- You are not connected to the present moment, and more likely connected to the past or future.
- You can get focused on what is negative or missing.
- You try to accomplish too many things.
- You can be disconnected from your body.

Being

- You connect with the present moment.
- You acknowledge and allow things to be as they are.
- You're open to pleasant, unpleasant and neutral emotions without judgment
- You have an inner sense of awareness, allowing peace, stillness and silence.
- You are very focused and attentive.
- You avoid multi-tasking.
- You increase cognitive effectiveness.

How Leaders Become More Mindfully Self-Aware

One thing that prevents leaders from engaging in mindfulness is the reticence to "let go of some things." Many leaders think "I can't let them down" or "it's my job to do those difficult things." Frequently these negative ideas or beliefs, or guilt, becomes dysfunctional. They all too often live in a world of "should" and "shouldn't."

A positive quality that can develop in leaders practicing mindfulness is appreciativeness. When leaders slow down and listen more actively and empathetically, often the result is the leaders' observation and attentiveness improves. As the research has shown, mindfulness helps people take a step back from their biases and stereotypes and be more open-minded.

The Research on Mindful Self-Aware Leadership

While much has been researched on the trait and state of mindfulness, including the benefits and impact on individuals, only recently have researchers turned their attention to mindfulness being incorporated into leadership style and leadership practices. The following describes some of the results of that research.

- Researchers have found leaders' trait of mindfulness was positively associated with employees' work-life balance, job satisfaction, citizenship behaviors, and job performance and negatively related to employee exhaustion and deviance.
- The results of several studies show mindfulness is positively associated with the overall score for leader flexibility, and with its two dualities: self-assertive and directive vs. collaborative and supportive, and long-term strategy vs. short-term execution.
- Researchers have suggested that mindfulness could help leaders respond more judiciously to the demands of their working environment rather than reacting impulsively to distractions or triggers, whether internal (e.g. thoughts, emotions) or external (practical constraints).
- Ruth Baer and her colleagues found mindfulness was related to behavioral flexibility--specifically, enhanced observing, describing, non-judging of inner experience, non-reactivity to inner experience and acting with awareness.

- Leading neuroscientists argue in their studies, that mindfulness enhances self-regulation through an increase in self-awareness.
- Researchers found in reviewing 30 research studies that mindfulness training changed brain structure and function associated with conscious decision making and emotional regulation and other functions.
- While conducting research for their book, *The Mind of the Leader*, Rasmus Hougaard and Jacqueline Carter interviewed more than 1,000 leaders and found that practicing mindfulness helped those leaders engage with their employees, create better connections and improve company performance.

Mindful Awareness is a Different Way of Conceptualizing Organizational Life

When our thoughts are turned inward like this we are engaged in what is termed metacognition. This common expression of this mode of processing helps us understand, solve or resolve what occupies the mind, especially when it has personal importance.

This process is primarily self-referential, in that we reflect on what is happening as it affects us. In addition, conceptual processing is frequently recurrent or repetitive, taking forms such as worry or rumination. In sum, conceptual processing involves interpreting stimuli and events in a way that is abstract, evaluative, and biased toward self-concerns."

In contrast, mindfulness is experiential processing, which involves attention to our internal state--thought or emotion--or devoting our attention to an external event itself through observation but not engagement. Experiential processing permits the individual to attend to a stimulus as it is, without immediate attempts to derive meaning from it. In experiential processing, mental images, self-talk, emotions, and impulses to act can be observed as part of the ongoing stream of consciousness.

This mindfulness experiential processing has been referred to as "decentering." For example, if we are confronted with an angry or abusive boss, through mindful awareness we can observe our internal experiences (cognitive, emotional, and physical), including how we may be interpreting the boss's anger or outburst, all in a detached and observational manner.

In experiential processing, our awareness of and attention to these reactions affords a degree of mental distance or disengagement,

The researchers explain, "With the capacity to witness events, thoughts, and emotions as they play out comes an ability to attend to occurrences as concrete phenomena rather than interpreting them in ways biased by personal memories, learned associations, or future projections."

Sustaining Mindful Self-Awareness in the Workplace

There's a multitude of ways in which workplace structures, systems and practices can easily incorporate mindfulness practices, which have been shown by research to be effective, and are incredibly cost effective. These practices are not so typical reorganizational or change management efforts, but rather a different way of viewing productivity, valuing people, and embracing the importance of quiet reflection, "doing nothing," focusing attention, being present focused, building emotional self-regulation and setting positive intentions for any activity.

Strategies and behaviors to sustain mindful self-awareness:

- **Remain completely focused when people talk to you.** During meetings, give your team your full attention. When an employee discusses a problem with you resist the urge to begin solving it in your head, or cut short the conversation with an answer, but instead listen without interruption or judgment.

- **Every day take a minute to stop whatever you are doing and practice mindful breathing.** Often when we are busy or stressed, our breathing changes by becoming shallower (or we even can hold our breath), which has a negative effect on brain function and blood pressure. An added practice can be feeling positive energy for each in-breath and letting go of stress with each out-breath.

- **Check your thoughts and particularly your emotions before a decision.** Every decision involves a certain level of bias; judgment and emotion. When you pause and bring awareness to your biases, judgments and emotions, you make better decisions. Mindfulness builds the awareness muscle in your head to mindfully regulate emotions, helping you better assess and make decisions without judgment.

- **Have a regular daily meditation practice.** Research has shown that meditating for 5-20 minutes each day can make a measurable difference in your leadership.

- **Emotionally ground yourself before you enter a room or a meeting, rather than rushing from one conversation or meeting directly into the other, without "cleansing" your mind of the residual thoughts or emotions from the previous encounter.** You could take a walk specifically to pause and re-center, also known as "walking meditation."

- **Break patterns such as multitasking, back-to-back meetings, and micromanaging.** These are all habits leaders participate in because they think they increase productivity.

13

How Humility Enhances Self-Awareness

"Humility is the base and foundation of all virtues, and without it, no other virtue can exist.*"*

Cervantes

We are hypocritical about the kind of leaders we need and the kind we have traditionally chosen and supported. Specifically, we have tended to choose the extroverts, the flamboyant narcissists, the psychopaths, the incompetents, and mostly men, far more often than we have chosen the quiet introverts, those with enhanced emotional intelligence, the effective, and humble. Yet, research shows that humble leaders are more effective and enjoy more positive relationships with others. Humility and self-awareness are interwoven like a tapestry.

What is Humility?

The term "humility" comes from the Latin word "humilitas," a noun related to the adjective "humilis," which may be translated as "humble", but also as "grounded", or "from the earth", since it derives from humus (earth). Humility gained a place of importance in various religions. The Bible (Philippians 2: 3-11) says "Do nothing from rivalry or conceit, but in humility count others more significant than yourselves." St. Augustine argued "It was pride that changed angels into devils; it is humility that makes men as angels."

In the Jewish tradition, humility is among the greatest of the virtues, and its opposite, pride, is among the worst of the vices. Moses, the greatest of men, is described as the humblest. In the Islamic religion being humble means that one is modest, submissive and respectful, not proud and arrogant. You lower yourself to the ground, not elevate yourself above others.

In prayer, Muslims prostrate themselves to the ground, acknowledging human beings' lowliness and humility before God. Like other spiritual traditions, Buddhism sees humility as a virtue. From a Buddhist perspective, humility is a result of enlightenment and nirvana. In the Buddhist text on Maha-karuna (great compassion), humility is one of the ten sacred qualities attributed to Avalokite Bodhisattva, or Buddha of Compassion.

Buddhism also advocates humility as a moral precept. Confucius said "Humility is the solid foundation of all virtues." Lao Tzu said "I have three precious things which I hold fast and prize. The first is gentleness; the second frugality; the third is humility, which keeps me from putting myself before others. Be gentle and you can be bold; be frugal and you can be liberal; avoid putting yourself before others and you can become a leader among men."

Hindus view humility as a spiritual and humanistic virtue. Ancient Hindu artists were never supposed to sign their names on their work, and temple artists, when creating statues of gods, are always supposed to leave a deliberate imperfection to show that they cannot really represent God.

—

Philosophers and spiritual sages have also identified humility as a "meta-virtue" that is foundational to other virtues such as forgiveness, courage, wisdom, and compassion.

Humility may be seen as foundational to other positive characteristics or a "temperance virtue" that guards against excess. Humility may temper other virtues, keeping them within the Aristotelian "golden mean" or the Buddhist "middle way"), and Confucian "zhongyong" ("doctrine of the mean). Humility prevents other characteristics from becoming extreme.

Non-Religious Perspectives on Humility Through the Ages

Outside of a religious context, humility is defined as being "unselved", a liberation from consciousness of self, a form of temperance that is neither having pride (or haughtiness) nor indulging in self-deprecation. Humility, in various interpretations is widely seen as a virtue which centers on low self-preoccupation, or unwillingness to put oneself forward, so it is in many religious and philosophical traditions, it contrasts with narcissism, hubris and other forms of pride and is an idealistic and rare intrinsic construct that has an extrinsic side.

Socrates said of humility: "Pride divides men, humility joins them." In describing the nature of virtuous self-knowledge as an appropriate attribute, Aristotle defined pride as respecting oneself. As with other virtues, Aristotle defined pride as the mean between a personal hubris and an insufficiency or a lack of self-esteem. In the *Nichomachean Ethics*, Aristotle explained that a person is proud if he both is and thinks of himself to be worthy of great things.

Both British philosopher David Hume and German philosopher Friedrich Nietzsche were critics of the trait of humility. Hume said "humility serves no manner of purpose; neither advance a man's fortune in the world, nor render him a more valuable member of society." German philosopher Frederick Nietzsche viewed humility as a strategy used by the weak to avoid being destroyed by the strong.

Mahatma Gandhi suggested that attempting to sustain truth without humility is doomed to become an "arrogant caricature" of truth. Albert Einstein said of humility, "I prefer an attitude of humility corresponding to the weakness of our intellectual understanding of nature and of our own being." And finally the esteemed writer C.S. Lewis said, "Humility is not thinking less of yourself, it's thinking of yourself less."

Unfortunately, our history has not been kind to the trait of humility. Dictionaries often describe humility as low self-esteem, self-degradation and meekness. In a 2016 College of Charleston survey, 56% of 5th and 6th graders said that the humble are embarrassed, sad, lonely or shy. When adults are asked to recount an experience of humility, they often tell a story about a time when they were publicly humiliated.

Characteristic Traits and Behaviors of Humble People

Researcher J.P. Tangney specified these features of humility: an accurate assessment of oneself; acknowledgement of one's limitations and mistakes; an openness to other perceptions and ideas; viewing one's accomplishments and abilities in perspective; lower self-focus; and appreciating other people and things.

Similarly, psychologist E. L. Worthington suggested that humility is reflected by traits such as being other-oriented, pro-social, altruistic, modest, willing to accept both strengths and weaknesses, and the absence of thoughts or behaviors that reflect being prideful, arrogant, or entitled. Humility tends to be associated with modesty.

Research on humility has shown that it is one of the core organizational virtues proposed to provide the foundation for moral action in the workplace and to foster positive behavior, exceptional performance, and altruism. In the context of organizations, virtues such as humility have been generally viewed as that which is good, human, and produces social betterment.

What Inhibits Humility?

Mark R. Leary and Chloe C. Banker argue in their book, *A Critical Examination and Reconceptualization of Humility,* "In contexts that operate as meritocracies, people who are good at something or who possess exceptional characteristics are entitled to preferential treatment within the domain of their expertise and accomplishments. The best athletes should get more playing time, the best employees should receive larger salaries, the best actors should win more awards, and so on. In general, norms often specify that people who accomplish and contribute the most may deserve additional recognition, respect, or deference in contexts in which their accomplishments and positive characteristics are relevant. Believing that one deserves to be treated as different or special in such contexts is normal and appropriate. "

Ryan Holiday, in his brilliant book, *Ego is the Enemy,* sees ego as the enemy of humility. He defines ego as "an unhealthy belief in our own importance." It is arrogance and self-centered ambition. "Ego is the voice that tells us we are better than we really are," Holiday says, "ego inhibits true success by preventing a direct and honest connection to the world around us."

Holiday blames our culture for fanning the flames of ego in our leaders: "Now more than ever, our culture fans the flames of ego. It's never been easier to talk, to puff ourselves up. We can brag about our goals to millions of our fans and followers. We can follow and interact with our idols on Twitter and Facebook. We can read books and sites and watch TED Talks; and drink from a fire hose of inspiration and validation like never before from self-help gurus. We can name ourselves CEO of our exists-only-on-paper company, We can announce big new on social media and let the congratulations roll in. We can publish articles about ourselves in outlets that used to be sources of objective journalism and stories of fact."

Our culture tells us to believe we are special; to think big; to be memorable; and to "dare greatly." We believe our success has to contain a bold vision or some revolutionary plan. We witness the radical risk-taking boasting of successful people in the media and try desperately to emulate it. As Holiday says, ego tries to "reverse engineer the right attitude, the right pose."

Great humble leaders were not aggressive, entitled, or constantly aware of their greatness, Holiday argues. They are confident but not arrogant: "Ego is the wicked sister of success."

Jennifer Cole Wright in her edited book, *Humility*, says, "The central problem with low humility is not that people think that they are better than others. People low in humility expect others to treat them as special; try to reap social benefits that they don't deserve; and their sense of entitlement leads them to behave in self-centered ways that disadvantage other people." In contrast, humble people who do not put themselves above others, or expect preferential treatment, or think they are entitled to a disproportionate share of any benefits are more likely to treat others in an egalitarian, respectful, and fair manner, Wright argues.

Are Certain Personality Types Predisposed to be Humbler?

Are people naturally predisposed to be humble? Humility would not have become possible until our pre-human ancestors acquired a sophisticated ability for symbolic self-relevant thought that allowed them to consider whether they should be treated specially because of their attributes or accomplishments. Scientists do not know for certain when our capacity for self-reflection first arose, as no evidence of it appears in the archeological record until less than 100,000 years ago, so humility as a component of self-reflection is a much more recent human attribute.

How Humility Reinforces Greater Self-Awareness

Humility entails an unvarnished and honest assessment of who you are. Humility is necessary to eliminate our self-oriented tendency to view others as inferior, or not worthy of our compassion or kindness. In this way, humility quiets the incessant push and pull of our desires, wishes, and fears, deepens our capacity for patience, moderation, and modesty.

Others writers have defined humility in terms of more of a focus on others than ourselves, encouraging the development of our empathy, gentleness, respect, and an appreciation for the equality, autonomy and value of others, as well as a concern for their welfare and a willingness to share credit for accomplishments with others. Humility can be seen as a virtue and opposite to a number of negative personality traits, including arrogance, vanity, conceit, egotism, grandiosity, pretentiousness, snobbishness, impertinence,

---

89

haughtiness, self-righteousness, domination, selfish ambition, and self-complacency.

How and when is humility cultivated? Some writers would argue through early life experience--experiencing "limbic resonance," humble people have a healthy sense of both autonomy and belonging through secure attachment, with caregivers and community members. When raised in a community and culture that fosters the formation of early emotional connectedness with and deep concern for others, humility will likely also begin to develop early, since the self-oriented biases that emerge as a function of our natural centeredness are being quieted through these social practices and are therefore not given the opportunity to manifest into self-absorption or self-worship.

The Research on Humble Leaders

As organizational environments have become more dynamic, uncertain and unpredictable, it becomes increasingly difficult for any one leader to "figure it all out of the top," says management guru Peter Senge. As a result, an emphasis has shifted to leaders engaging in more "bottom-up," humble approaches to leadership.

Although a great deal of disagreement about the precise leader behaviors that are associated with humility exists, there is some consensus that humility generally involves how leaders tend to view themselves more objectively, others more appreciatively, and new information or ideas more openly.

Humility is mainly an innate virtue or stable personality trait, rather than a set of behaviors that leaders can enact. For instance, some writers have suggested that leader humility involves self-awareness, openness to new ideas, and the tendency to look past or "transcend" oneself. Similarly, others have argued that humility entails a willingness to understand the self (strengths and weaknesses) and an orientation toward others more than self.

In stark contrast with narcissism, which is often described as entailing volatile swings from grandiose to self-abasing self-views, humility has been labeled as a temperance virtue that has a stabilizing or grounding influence on self-perceptions. Thus, though humility and narcissism are likely to be negatively related, a humble leader is not merely the opposite of a narcissistic one. In addition, since the strong negative emotions of envy and jealousy often hinder the ability to make accurate self-appraisals, scholars have suggested that effective emotional management and awareness are associated with humility.

Researchers Yanhan Zhu and colleagues studied the relationship between humble leadership and employee resilience and productivity and concluded:

- Humble leaderships can be defined as: a leadership style in which a leader evaluates him/herself and subordinates through a multifaceted and objective lens, appreciating subordinates' positive worth, strengths, and contributions. It contains three behavioral components: (a) a willingness to acknowledge one's limits and mistakes; (b) shining a spotlight on employees' contributions and strengths; and (c) keeping openness to advice, ideas, and feedback.
- Humble leadership is perceived by employees as a way to facilitate personal and professional growth.

Edgar H. Schein and Peter A. Schein in their research and a published study, *Humble Leadership: The Power of Relationships,*

Openness and Trust, argue that the growing complexity of the modern world requires stronger workplace relationships in order to accomplish tasks. They argue the pace of change in the world is increasing in just about every context. Schein and Schein cite examples where humble leadership has been developed: The country of Singapore and the U.S. Military.

The authors argue that the changing world necessitates humble leadership due to the changing nature of work. Leadership will become more and more about context and process rather than content and expertise. They argue that humble leadership can help facilitate the movement toward agile organizations.

The authors make the salient point that the workplace now puts a premium on so-called "soft-skills" and experimental learning, and is moving away from authoritarian and one-size fits all training and development.

Humble leaders are more effective and better liked, according to a study published in the *Academy of Management Journal.* "Leaders of all ranks view admitting mistakes, spotlighting follower strengths and modelling "teachability" as being at the core of humble leadership" says Bradley Owens, assistant professor of organization and human resources at the University at Buffalo School of Management. A follow-up study published in the journal *Organization Science,* using data from more than 700 employees and 218 leaders, confirmed that leader humility is associated with more learning-oriented teams, more engaged employees and lower voluntary employee turnover.

The more honesty and humility an employee may have, the higher their job performance, as rated by the employees' supervisor according to a Baylor University study published in the journal

Personality and Individual Differences by Wade Rowatt, associate professor of psychology and neuroscience. He found humility was a unique predictor of job performance. "In fact, we found that humility and honesty not only correspond with job performance, but it predicted job performance above and beyond any of the other five personality traits like agreeableness and conscientiousness," Rowatt says.

Amy Y. Ou and her colleagues at Arizona State University published a study in *Administrative Science Quarterly*, examining the leadership traits associated with Confucianism. Those traits include self-awareness, openness to feedback, and a focus on the greater good and others' welfare, as opposed to dwelling on oneself. Ou and her colleagues argue the self-awareness of humble leaders enables them to be open-minded and willing to learn, to appreciate both their own strengths and weaknesses as well as those of others, and to transcend the self in the pursuit of a higher and more significant objective while continuing to improve.

In an article in the *Harvard Business Review* entitled "Level 5 Leadership: The Triumph of Humility and Fierce Resolve," leadership expert Jim Collins argues the best leaders exhibit humility, compelling modesty, shunning public adulation and are never boastful. In a widely read *Harvard Business Review* publication, Collins explained that the personal humility of Level 5 Leaders was typified by: A compelling modesty about their accomplishments; quiet determination rather than charisma; ambition focused on the company rather than self; willingness to accept personal responsibility for failures; and acknowledgment of the role of others in achieving success.

Joseph Folkman writing in a new report, "How Do You Become an Effective Leader? Stay Humble?", a follow up to a previous article on humble leaders in *Harvard Business Review,* argues "How do people make the judgment that a leader is arrogant or humble? Arrogant leaders don't parade around with a badge indicating they are conceited. Yet, there is a high degree of consensus within organizations about who is humble and who is arrogant. The reality is that there are a set of very predictable behaviors that send clear signals about an individual's humility or arrogance." Folkman studied 1,072 leaders and concluded the following:

- **Humble leaders are rated higher than arrogant leaders on an overall leadership effectiveness index**. A comparison of arrogant and humble leaders on an overall leadership effectiveness index composed of 54 behaviors that differentiate the most effective from the least effective leaders. Arrogant leaders were rated at the 34th percentile, while humble leaders were rated at the 66th percentile.
- **Humble leaders demonstrated that people are just as important as results**. Arrogant leaders believe that results are the ultimate goal, and if a few people get negatively affected, that's just the cost of doing business. Humble leaders understand the balance of achieving while still being sensitive to individual needs. They also believe if you take care of people, they will be more engaged and dedicated, which will produce better results in the long run.
- **Humble leaders focused on gaining trust from others.** Humble leaders do everything they can to build up trust with others. They are more effective on the key levers that build trust, which are: creating positive relationships,

consistently delivering on their promises, and providing expertise and good judgment.

- **Humble leaders believe that success comes from cooperation and collaboration.** Arrogant leaders believe that they can accomplish goals on their own. They resist collaboration because they want all the credit for themselves. The humble leaders know that organizational success comes from people working together. They ask others for help and resist taking credit for the accomplishments of others.

- **Humble leaders are role models and walk their talk.** When humble leaders ask others to do something, they make sure they do it first. Arrogant leaders are okay with asking others to do what they do not do. They are fine with having a double standard, or perhaps they don't see it. In many ways they act as though they are a privileged class where rules for others do not apply to them.

- **Humble leaders ask for and act on feedback from others.** Humble leaders ask others for feedback and work hard to implement their suggestions for change. Arrogant leaders feel that they do not want or need feedback from others. In fact, they often feel that asking for feedback would signal a lack of confidence in themselves. Therefore, they resist asking.

- **Humble leaders resolve conflicts productively.** Arrogant leaders tend to create conflict with others. This is due in part to a belief that conflict is a good thing that fuels competitive energy from others. Humble leaders feel that conflict creates a negative work environment and work hard to resolve conflicts.

- **Humble leaders give others honest feedback.** The arrogant leaders believe their job is to be the judge and let others know when they make mistakes. Their feedback is almost always negative and corrective. The humble leader realizes that honest feedback needs to reflect an individual's performance.

Folkman says the behaviors listed above represent the largest differences between arrogant and humble leaders. "Looking over the list," Folkman says, "it isn't difficult to realize why humble leaders win. In many ways, humble leaders believe that leadership is the ability to get work done through others. In contrast, arrogant leaders believe leadership is the ability to get work done by others."

Humility and Our Concept of Leadership

Increasingly, scholars and practitioners have argued the need for today's leaders to approach their roles with more humility. As a result of workplace complexity and fast changes requiring leader flexibility, recent leadership theories have begun to place greater emphasis on the bottom-up aspects of leadership. Some experts even argue for a need to change "the very idea of leadership—what it is and how it works and even how people even know it when they see it."

Researchers have also suggested that leaders should move beyond the hero myth or "great man" theory of leadership by having leaders show their humanness by being open about their limitations in knowledge and experience, and focusing more on how followers influence the process of leadership.

More recently many scholars and experts have called for professionals and leaders in all professions to approach their roles with more humility. For example, for lawyers and judges, humility is important to effectively interpret the law and balance the ideals of justice and mercy. In medicine, competence and humility are seen as the two essential dimensions of medical professionalism. Humility has also been spot-lighted as important for political and military leaders, particularly in the current political climate.

Bottom-up, participative leadership lends itself to the inclusion of humble leadership. Although some advocate top-down strategic change approaches, others are now arguing the need for organizations to learn to "grow strategy from below," seek bottom-up "small wins," as reflected in the agile leadership model. Advocates of emergent change argue the importance of organizations being willing to live on the "edge of chaos" to achieve the level of flexibility and adaptability required for continuous transformation.

There are several similarities between humble leadership theory and servant leader theory, a general focus on development being the most obvious. Servant leaders "view the development of followers as an end, in and of itself, not merely a means to reach the leader's or the organization's goals."

Both the research and my three decades of coaching and mentoring leaders has led me to conclude the following about why humble leadership is desirable:

- Humble leaders are more effective.
- Employees working for humble leaders are more engaged, satisfied and productive and better organizational citizens. Humble leaders give credit to their team members and let everyone share in the team's success.
- Humble leaders build trust.

- Humble leaders recognize their own shortcomings and are willing to ask for help when a problem is outside of their area of expertise.
- Humble leaders are coachable. They listen to feedback from others and use it to improve their own performance.

Humble Self-Aware Leaders Are Often Overlooked

Unfortunately, modern organizations often overlook humble leaders. Charisma, charm and self-proclamations of competence are still seen as desirable leadership traits, and predominate recruitment strategies, despite their lack of association with leadership effectiveness. Because humble leaders give credit to others and avoid the spotlight, senior leadership often overlooks and underestimates their accomplishments. Research shows the following.

A Lack of Humility Ruins Organizations

Most businesses ultimately fail due to poor leadership. There are several persistent themes that can account for leadership failure and all are related to a lack of humility. The first theme of poor management is an exaggerated sense of self and entitlement, often exhibited by narcissistic leaders. Such narcissists obviously lack humility but are quite adept at getting themselves into leadership positions. Ultimately, these leaders alienate their employees because they make promises that they cannot keep, they take credit for all successes, and they blame anyone and everyone else for any failures.

The second theme of poor management is a lack of awareness about how one's actions are affecting others. These leaders are insensitive to the "people side" of doing business. Further, they fail to recognize this insensitivity as a shortcoming. While humble leaders are open to listening to what other people feel and think, insensitive leaders are unwilling to listen to opinions and feedback from others.

The third theme of poor management is an exaggerated need for social support and approval. Narcissistic leaders and those with low humility are in constant need of positive reinforcement, praise and personal loyalty. Similarly, the fourth theme of poor management is insecurity and low self-confidence. Both of these traits are rooted in insecurity and fear of rejection. Leaders who lack humility are desperate for attention and approval of others. Indeed, much of their expressed arrogance and overconfidence is intended to mask a deep desire for the approval of others. Leaders who are appropriately humble are seen as confident and suffer from neither diffidence nor arrogance.

Leaders are the most consequential members of any organization. Unfortunately, the current cultural attraction to leaders who are charming, charismatic and self-promoting (e.g., transformational leadership) is leading us in the wrong direction. Some of our most effective leaders are hiding in our organizations, masked by their own humility. For the future success of our organizations, finding them is critical.

Humility can be a powerful force in enhancing and developing leader self-awareness. They go hand in glove.

14

How Doing Nothing Helps You Be More Self-Aware

"Idleness is not just a vacation, an indulgence or a vice; it is as indispensable to the brain as vitamin D is to the body, and deprived of it we suffer a mental affliction as disfiguring as rickets."

Tim Kreider

When was the last time you found doing absolutely nothing and thought, "This is really fantastic, I really wish I could do nothing all of the time." Doing nothing doesn't mean that you're just doing something that isn't work or school related, like watching Netflix or eating ice cream, doing nothing means that you're alone by yourself with nothing but your thoughts coming and going like the clouds passing with the breeze. Think again now, when was the last time you were doing absolutely nothing that you didn't think, "I should really be doing something productive."

According to a scientific study, some people would rather get an electric shock than be alone with their thoughts and do nothing. Shocking, isn't it, to think that we as Americans would rather be in pain than run the risk of having to do nothing?

101

Hence the popularity of brainless smartphone apps that allow users to tap out of the wrestling match of our minds and succumb instead to the mind-numbing effect of technology. But playing Angry Birds isn't "doing nothing," it's avoiding doing nothing, and that's dangerous.

Somewhere along the way North American society gave up on notions such as relaxation, idleness, and living in the moment as an important part of daily life. Having periods of time with little activity has always been a part of life and was assuredly accepted and enjoyed by your ancestors in a way that has been long forgotten. It never had to be defined, until now. It is easy to be consumed by "shoulds" and "musts." It is easy to forget some of your most basic needs and, along with them, the most basic ways of fulfilling them.

In the article, published in *Perspectives in Psychological Science,* a journal of the Association for Psychological Science, Mary Helen Immordino-Yang, a professor of education, psychology and neuroscience at the University of Southern California. and her colleagues surveyed the existing scientific literature from neuroscience and psychological science, exploring what it means when our brains are at rest.

In recent years, researchers have explored the idea of rest by looking at the so-called "default mode" network of the brain, a network that is noticeably active when we are resting and focused inward. Findings from these studies suggest that individual differences in brain activity during rest are correlated with components of socio-emotional functioning, such as self-awareness and moral judgment, as well as different aspects of learning and memory. Immordino-Yang and her colleagues believe that research on the brain at rest can yield important insights into the importance of reflection and quiet time for learning.

"We focus on the outside world in education and don't look much at inwardly focused reflective skills and attentions, but inward focus impacts the way we build memories, make meaning and transfer that learning into new contexts," says Immordino-Yang, "What are we doing in schools to support kids turning inward?"

Accumulated research suggests that the networks that underlie a focus inward versus outward likely are interdependent, and our ability to regulate and move between them probably improves with maturity and practice. While outward attention is essential for carrying out tasks and learning from classroom lessons, for example, the reflection and consolidation that may accompany mind wandering is equally important, fostering healthy development and learning in the longer term.

"Balance is needed between outward and inward attention, since time spent mind wandering, reflecting and imagining may also improve the quality of outward attention that kids can sustain," says Immordino-Yang.

She and her colleagues argue that mindful introspection can become an effective part of the classroom curriculum, providing students with the skills they need to engage in constructive internal processing and productive reflection. Research indicates that when children are given the time and skills necessary for reflecting, they often become more motivated, less anxious, perform better on tests, and plan more effectively for the future.

And mindful reflection is not just important in an academic context --it's also essential to our ability to make meaning of the world around us. Inward attention is an important contributor to the development of moral thinking and reasoning and is linked with overall socio-emotional well-being.

Immordino-Yang and her colleagues worry that the high attention demands of fast-paced urban and digital environments may be systematically undermining opportunities for young people to look inward and reflect, and that this could have negative effects on their psychological development. This is especially true in an age when social media seems to be a constant presence in teens' day-to-day lives.

"Consistently imposing overly high-attention demands on children, either in school, through entertainment, or through living conditions, may rob them of opportunities to advance from thinking about 'what happened' or 'how to do this' to constructing knowledge about 'what this means for the world and for the way I live my life,'" Immordino-Yang writes.

According to the authors, perhaps the most important conclusion to be drawn from research on the brain at rest is the fact that all rest is not idleness. While some might be inclined to view rest as a wasted opportunity for productivity, the authors suggest that constructive internal reflection is critical for learning from past experiences and appreciating their value for future choices, allowing us to understand and manage ourselves in the social world.

Although modern Western society tends to emphasize the importance of willpower and striving, there are some central human goals--happiness, relaxation, charisma--that appear to come only to those who are not trying to achieve them. The importance of "not trying" was recognized by early Chinese thinkers, who understood how relaxed spontaneity could lead to both personal and social success. The early Chinese ideal of effortless action is also looking increasingly plausible from the perspective of modern psychology, as we come to better understand the pervasive role of embodied, tacit knowledge in human behavior.

Although there were certainly thinkers in early China advocating rationality and self-control, the mainstream thinkers--the Confucians and Daoists who set the tone for the subsequent 2000 years of East Asian intellectual history--believed that true moral perfection and spiritual fulfilment required attaining a state where striving is transcended.

The ideal of "effortless action", or *wu-wei*, refers to the dynamic, unselfconscious state of mind of a person who is optimally active and effective. People in wu-wei feel as if they are doing nothing, while at the same time they might be creating a brilliant work of art, smoothly negotiating a complex social situation, or even bringing the entire world into harmonious order.

The distinctive feature of wu-wei, on the other hand, is a sense of immersion in a greater, shared and valued whole. So, although wu-wei can be attained in challenging situations requiring skill or training, it is more commonly encountered in less adrenaline-inducing activities, like a quiet walk in a special landscape, a simple meal with family and friends, or just sitting on a beach watching the ocean roll in. Wu-wei is fundamentally about belonging and meaning, not skill or challenge per se.

That said, these days we do seem to live in a society dead-set against spontaneity. We've got three year-olds attending drill sessions to get an edge on admission to the best preschool, and then growing into hyper-competitive high school students popping Ritalin to enhance their test results and keep up with a brutal schedule of afterschool activities. As adults, our personal and professional lives increasingly revolve around a relentless quest for greater efficiency and higher productivity, crowding out leisure time and simple unstructured pleasures. The result is that too many of us spend our days stumbling around tethered "umbilically" to our smartphones, immersed in an endless stream of competitive games, e-mails, texts, tweets, dings, pings and pokes, getting up too early, staying up too late, never far from the bright glow of tiny LCD screens.

It doesn't need to be this way, though, and in fact this incessant effort and striving are often profoundly counterproductive. Many of our most desired goals--happiness, attractiveness, spontaneity--are best pursued indirectly, and conscious thought and effortful striving actually interfere with their attainment.

This is a fact that is slowly being more appreciated. Recent studies have suggested that non-stop exam prep and a dearth of unstructured playtime is having a negative impact on children's emotional and cognitive development. In business management, there's a growing recognition that pushing harder too often leads to producing less, and that people who put themselves last, in the sense of generously helping others, actually end up ahead in the long run.

Stephanie Brown, author of *Speed: Facing Our Addiction to Fast and Faster—And Overcoming Our Fear of Slowing Down*, argues we are addicted to busyness and accept it as a norm: "There's this widespread belief that thinking and feeling will only slow you down and get in your way but it's the opposite." She argues, and most psychotherapists would contend, that suppressing negative feelings only gives them more power, leading to intrusive thoughts, which can prompt people to be even busier to avoid them.

Manfred Ket De Vries, INSEAD Distinguished Professor of Leadership development and Organizational Change, writing in INSEAD Knowledge argues, "In today's networked society we are at risk of becoming victims of interaction overload. Introspection and reflection have become lost arts as the temptation to 'just finish this' or 'find out that' is often too great to risk." De Vries argues that working harder is not working smarter and in fact, setting aside regular periods of "doing nothing" may be "the best thing we can do to induce states of mind that nurture our imagination and improve our mental health."

De Vries contends that "doing nothing" has become unacceptable. People associate it with irresponsibility, and wasting valuable time. It doesn't provide the stimulation that busyness and distraction-inducing behaviors like constantly checking emails, Facebook and texting do. The biggest danger, he says, is not so much that we lose connection with each other, but with ourselves.

In our cyber age, where we have almost limitless selection of entertainment and distraction, it's become easier to be in a constant state of busyness than it is to do nothing. The myriad of our activities and world of multi-tasking deludes us that we are actually being more productive. The problem is we have lost the knowledge of balancing action with reflection. And the result can be psychological burnout.

Leaders in organizations are much to blame. Work addicts are highly encouraged, supported and rewarded. Yet, study after study shows there is not a causal relationship between working hard and working smart. In fact, a workaholic environment can actually not only contribute to significant personal and mental health problems but productivity can actually decline.

We seem to have forgotten a long history of belief and practice that doing nothing is a valuable opportunity to stimulate unconscious creative and innovating thinking. We need time to incubate our thinking. Doing nothing can be one of the best ways to deal with complex issues.

In the scientific journal *Nature,* author Kerri Smith reviews the brain research regarding the importance of downtime and doing nothing. In a resting "do nothing" state, the brain is not doing nothing. It is completing the unconscious tasks of integrating and process conscious experiences.

Other studies suggest that not giving yourself time to reflect impairs one's ability to empathize with others. The more in touch we are with our feelings and inner experiences, the more accurate and compassionate we become about what others are experiencing.

Tim Kreider wrote in *The New York Times.* "The space and quiet that idleness provides is a necessary condition for standing back from life and seeing it whole, for making unexpected connections and waiting for the wild summer lightning strikes of inspiration--it is, paradoxically, necessary to getting any work done."

Researchers have found that resting minds are creative minds. Numerous studies have shown that people tend to develop more novel, inventive and innovative ideas if they allow their minds to wander rather focus narrowly on one task. Some companies such as Google recognized this fact and provide professional growth courses such as "Search Inside Yourself," and "Neural Self-Hacking," and also mindfulness meditation where the goal is to recognize and accept inner thoughts and feelings rather than avoiding or repressing them.

K. Anders Ericsson, a professor of psychology at Florida State University, conducted a study in Berlin and found that the amount of time successful musicians spent practicing each day was surprisingly low--a mere 90 minutes per day. In fact, the most successful musicians not only practiced less, but also took more naps throughout the day and indulged in breaks during practice when they grew tired or stressed.

In a recent thought-provoking review of research on the default mode network, Mary Helen Immordino-Yang of the University of Southern California and her co-authors argue that when we are resting the brain is anything but idle and that, far from being purposeless or unproductive, downtime is in fact essential to mental processes that affirm our identities, develop our understanding of human behavior and instil an internal code of ethics--processes that depend on the default mode network (DMN).

Related research suggests that the default mode network is more active and some studies have demonstrated that the mind obliquely solves tough problems while daydreaming—an experience many people have had while taking a shower. Epiphanies may seem to come out of nowhere, but they are often the product of unconscious mental activity during downtime.

In my work as an executive and leadership coach, I stress the importance of developing the important habits of reflection time, energy renewal, "doing nothing," and working less which can actually result in greater productivity and certainly a more fulfilled life.

Practical Slowing Down Strategies and Habits

1. **Protect your focus time.** Block chunks of time on your work calendar for focusing on tasks that require intense concentration, and make it clear to others to not interrupt you. Doing so signals to others that you are serious about accomplishing specific goals and are therefore prioritizing the tasks needed to accomplish them.

2. **Seriously reduce or eliminate multitasking from your work routine.** Multitasking seriously reduced productivity. This includes the discipline of not being "on" all the time by checking your email and social media platforms.

3. **Vary the location of your work.** Taking your work offsite to give yourself a radically different experience that could spark some inspiration. If you work in a large city, take advantage of the myriad of public spaces such as parks, coffee shops and plazas that are accommodating to workers with plentiful seating and free Wi-Fi. A public setting can positively change your perspective and help you put things in broader context.

4. **Block in reflection time in your calendar.** Rather than always focusing on the immediate tasks of doing what is required or expected, block in a regular block of time each day or once a week to reflect without actually doing anything. Focus on your feelings, your long range goals or vision for the future, which uses a different creative part of your brain that is beneficial for satisfaction and stability.

5. **Eat mindfully.** Eating more mindfully can be a meditative practice. Chew every bite slowly, analyze tastes like you're a foodie, and generally savor the experience. Don't view eating as an interruption into your activity filled life and something

you need to finish quickly so you can get on with more important things.

6. **Do nothing when you wake up.** Rather than immediately jumping out of bed to shower and rush to work, or hurriedly checking your messages on your computer or phone, taking 10 or 15 minutes to just lie there and notice your thoughts without engaging with them, helps you ease into the day with calm.

7. **Stop overscheduling your family life.** More activities in the absence of quality slow time do not make for a better life either for you or your family. Having unscheduled, spontaneous and unplanned time for yourself and your family is critical to work-life balance.

8. **Learn how to say no.** Saying yes can open you up to new possibilities challenges, but saying yes all the time makes you needy and can reinforce an external source for your self-esteem. Saying no can give you a chance for me-time, an hour when you don't have to keep any commitments or please anyone else, or a half-hour when you can just kick back and do absolutely nothing.

9. **Walk more and drive less.** Park the car and try walking to different places. Walking is not wasting time and actually helps you improve your focus. Deliberately taking walks may reduce your time, but it forces you to slow down your thinking so you can focus when you need to.

15

Silence is Golden

"Thoughts emerge from the nothingness of silence. Words come out of the void. Your very essence emerged from emptiness. All creativity requires some stillness."

Wayne Dyer

The Healing Power of Silence

Our modern world is a noisy place, particularly in large cities, where most people live in Western countries. Silence is rare, yet, is of great value to the quality of our lives, and a fundamental part of the power of solitude.

A study by Professor Gary W. Evans from Cornell University, published in Psychological Science, charted the effects of airport noise on school children near Munich's airport. The study showed that children exposed to noise developed a stress response which actually caused them to ignore the noise. He found that the children ignored both the harmful noise of the airport, along with other more everyday noises, such as speech.

Silence is comforting, and nourishing. It can be inspirational. It nurtures the mind, body and soul. In contrast the noisy world is drowning out our creativity, our inner connection and hampering our resilience. Science is now showing that silence may be just what we need to regenerate our exhausted brains and bodies.

Studies show that noise has a powerful physical effect on our brains, causing elevated levels of stress hormones. Sound travels to the brain as electrical signals via the ear. Even when we are sleeping these sound waves cause the body to react and activate the amygdala, the part of the brain associated with memory and emotion, leading to the release of stress hormones. So, living in a consistently noisy environment will cause you to experience extremely high levels of these harmful hormones.

The word noise comes from the Latin word NAUSIA, (nausea) or the Latin word NOXIA, meaning hurt, damage or injury. Studies have shown that noise has been linked to high blood pressure, heart disease, tinnitus and loss of sleep. More and more people are unable to function in noisy environments. And now science has the proof not only that noise hurts, but also that silence heals.

Many meditation teachers and spiritual teachers advise students to take frequent meditative silent pauses throughout the day. Though we may think of silence as a lack of input, science says otherwise. Research by a Duke University regenerative biologist, Imke Kirste, discovered that two hours of silence per day prompted cell development in the hippocampus, the brain region related to the formation of memory, involving the senses.

Taking Time to Unplug

According to Attention Restoration Theory, when you are in an environment with lower levels of sensory input, the brain can "recover" some of its cognitive abilities. With our digital world, our brains get less time to switch off. We are constantly processing enormous amounts of information. Research has shown the constant attention demands of modern life is placing a lot of stress on our prefrontal cortex--the part of the brain responsible for making decisions, solving problems and more. When we spend time alone in silence, our brains are able to relax and release this constant focus.

Researchers found that while noise creates stress, silence relieves stress and tension in the brain and body. Noise makes us lose our concentration, cognitive powers and causes decreased motivation and brain functioning, but studies show that spending some time in silence can amazingly restore what was lost through exposure to excessive noise. The ancient spiritual masters have known this all along; silence heals, silence takes us deeply into ourselves, and silence balances the body and mind. Now science is saying the same thing.

According to a 2006 study in *Heart*, two minutes of silence relieves tension in the body and brain and is more relaxing than listening to music. This was attributed to changes in blood pressure and blood circulation in the brain.

A 2013 study published in the journal *Brain Structure and Function* found two hours of silence could create new cells in the hippocampus region. This is essential since the hippocampus is linked to our ability to learn, remember things, and even our emotions.

There are retreats that promote the power of silence by refraining from reading, writing, or eye contact. One hundred scientists went on a retreat for research and found shutting off speech heightens awareness in other areas.

Silence May Also Help in the Following Ways:

- **Creativity.** During silence you can allow your thoughts to go where they will. Many people subsequently find inspiration arises. Solutions to current or long-standing problems may suddenly occur to you, or you find an innovative solution. Alternative ideas could coalesce, and you may think of ideas that never occurred to you before.

- **Awareness of self and environment.** In silence, you may notice a distinct shift in your ability to be more self-aware or the emotions or feelings that arise. Or you may be more aware of your immediate environment and notice things you didn't before.

- **Reflection.** Silence permits the kind of reflection that promotes the ability to connect threads in a seemingly disorganized, disconnected world. Or after meditating in silence, you may be more motivated to mend significant relationships that have become strained.

- **Insomnia.** In a 2015 study published in *JAMA Internal Medicine*, older adults experiencing insomnia found relief in the form of improved sleep quality and less daytime impairment after undergoing a 6-week intervention of silent mindfulness meditation.

16

The Power of Solitude

"There is a pleasure in the pathless woods,
There is a rapture on the lonely shore,
There is society, where none intrudes,
By the deep sea, and music in its roar:
I love not man the less, but Nature more"
Lord Byron

When was the last time you had meaningful time alone? No meetings, no appointment? No phone calls? No headphones on listening to music? No distractions of any kind?

Technology has profoundly changed our relationships with other people, with time, with how we live our lives. Yet, the biggest impact has been in our relationship with ourselves which transcends all other relationships.

Being with ourselves is not enough. We see ourselves as a void to be filled - with entertainment, information, or with possessions. We think being alone is the same as loneliness.

Our own company is not good enough, we have to be with others. While we are waiting for a taxi, or transit or the doors to an event to open, we check our phone to make sure we haven't missed anything, or we feel we must connect with someone.

I'm reminded of the scene in the movie Christmas Vacation, where Chevy Chase's boss is sitting alone at a huge table, and he picks up the phone and barks at his assistant "Get me someone . . . and get me someone while I'm waiting." We're embarrassed to sit at a table in a café or restaurant by ourselves, afraid that people will think we don't deserve company or don't have any friends. Anything but just being quietly with ourselves. We relate to ourselves as the hole at the center of the donut.

While some would argue that it's possible to become more self-aware during the course of our daily activities, or in the company of others, I would argue that solitude and stillness are necessary to fully achieve desirable self-awareness. Many people have lost their capacity and desire to experience solitude and stillness, and therefore, are damaging their self-awareness.

Artists, musicians, leaders and everyday people throughout history have embraced solitude, stillness and quiet as both a way of replenishing their souls and feeding their creative inspiration.

In 1840, the English writer Edgar Allan Poe described what he called the "mad energy" of a man who wandered the streets of London from dusk till dawn desperately searching for human interaction. His despair could be temporarily relieved only by immersing himself in a boisterous throng of people. "He refuses to be alone," Poe wrote, "he is the man of the crowd."

Like many writers and philosophers through the ages, Poe stressed the significance of reflection in solitude. It was "such a great misfortune", he wrote, "to lose the capacity to be alone with oneself, to get caught up in the crowd, to surrender one's singularity to mind-numbing conformity."

Writing about the importance of solitude, Ralph Waldo Emerson quoted Pythagoras: "In the morning, – solitude … that nature may speak to the imagination, as she does never in company." Emerson encouraged teachers to press upon their pupils the importance of "periods and habits of solitude," habits that made "serious and abstracted thought" possible.

The idea of solitude also occupied Hannah Arendt, a German-Jewish émigré who fled Nazism and found refuge in the United States. She wrote that solitude empowered the individual to "contemplate her actions and develop her conscience, to escape the cacophony of the crowd – to finally hear herself think."

Arendt recognized that: "A person who does not know that silent intercourse (in which we examine what we say and what we do) will not mind contradicting himself, and this means he will never be either able or willing to account for what he says or does; nor will he mind committing any crime, since he can count on its being forgotten the next moment."

Arendt believed that society could function freely and democratically only if it were made up of individuals engaged in reflection in solitude. Arendt said that "living together with others begins with living together with oneself".

Solitude is Not the Same as Loneliness

Philosophers made a distinction between solitude and loneliness. In *The Republic*, Plato describes how Socrates celebrates the solitary philosopher. In the allegory of the cave, Plato describes how the philosopher escapes from the darkness of an underground den-- and from being alone but not lonely, the philosopher becomes attuned the world by being attuned to his inner self.

In our always on, instantaneous, digital hyper-connected world we rarely create space for solitary contemplation. We check our email or text and phone messages hundreds of times per day; we obsessively thumb scan our Twitter, Facebook and Instagram, aching to connect with others. We search through social media for friends, and friends of friends, colleagues and business contacts, celebrities and people we barely know. For what purpose? Connection and companionship?

Solitude is not just a physical state of mind essential to the development of our inner life, it's also a practice that prepares us for participation in social and political life. To keep meaningful company with others, we must learn to keep meaningful company with ourselves. Sages and inventors understood this. The Buddhists talk of "walking meditation," or "kinhin," a long session of sitting, particularly in nature, stimulating both calm and creativity. Danish philosopher Kierkegaard wrote while he was walking alone. The German philosopher Fredrich Nietzsche claimed the ideas in his classic *Thus Spoke Zarathustra* came to him on a long walk by himself.

Genius inventor Nikola Tesla made his discovery of the rotating magnetic field on a walk by himself through a park in Budapest. When he lived in Paris, American writer Ernest Hemingway took long walks along the river to inspire his writing. Solitary walks were also part of the daily schedules for Charles Darwin, Steve Jobs, Martin Luther King Jr., Walt Whitman and Ludwig van Beethoven. Bill Gates has twice a year taken what he calls "think week" where he spends seven days alone in a cabin in the forest. During that time, he reads and thinks.

So how do we deal with the problem of information overload, Mike Erwin asks in his article in *Harvard Business Review*: "There is no silver bullet to solving the complex problems ushered in by the information age. But there are some good places to start, and one of them is counterintuitive - solitude. Having the discipline to step back from the noise of the world is essential to staying focused. This is even more important in a highly politicized society that constantly incites our emotions, causing the cognitive effects of distractions to linger. We need solitude, a state of mind, a space in which to focus one's own thoughts without distraction — and where the mind can work through a problem on its own."

The Psychology of Solitude

Anthony Storr, a prominent psychiatrist, scholar and Emeritus Fellow at Green College, Oxford, wrote a brilliant book, *Solitude: A Return to the Self*. He analyzes the topic of solitude, particularly from the perspective of the lives of famous creative people:

- "Gibbon [Edward, author of the *Rise and Fall of the Roman Empire*,] is surely right. The majority of poets, novelists, composers and to a lesser extent, of painters and sculptors, are bound to spend a great deal of their time alone."
- "It is widely believed that interpersonal relationships of an intimate kind are the chief, if not the only, source of human happiness. Yet the lives of creative individuals often seem to run counter to this assumption…. For example, this is true of Descartes, Newton, Locke, Pascal, Spinoza, Kant, Schopenhauer, Nietzsche, Kierkegaard and Wittgenstein."

Storr argues that "The capacity to be alone thus becomes linked with self-discovery and self-realization; with becoming aware of one's deepest needs, feelings and impulses."

The brain engages in important integration processes while we are asleep and when we are in quiet solitude, Storr contends, based on his examination of brain research. He says that the capacity to be alone is a valuable resource when changes of mental attitude are required, as well. After major alternations in circumstances, fundamental reappraisal of the significant and meaning of existence may be needed. Storr says: "In a culture in which interpersonal relationships are generally considered to provide the answer to every form of distress, it is sometimes difficult to persuade well-meaning helpers that solitude can be as therapeutic as emotional support."

Echoing the observations of other experts in human behavior our digital world, Storr contends that "western culture makes the peace of solitude difficult to attain;" and, "noise is so ubiquitous that many people evidently feel uncomfortable in its absence."

Solitude and still go hand in glove. If you've ever quietly and easily solved a problem in seconds or minutes that you've been wrestling with for weeks or months, then suddenly feel a quiet within, that's a stillness. Or if you've walked alone in the park among the trees or along the beach, and feel a quiet calmness come over you, that's stillness.

Leaders need those moments of stillness, only achieved by quiet solitude, to develop a clear sense of what action or decision to make next, particularly in a crisis. Their capacity for self-awareness expands.

During the many crises President John F. Kennedy faced, he often sought solitude in the White House Rose Garden; went for long swims; or sat in his specially made rocking chair in the Oval Office, bathed in the light of those enormous windows, easing his chronic back pain.

The chaos of modern life means we often don't live in the present moment. Instead, we habitually try to get out of it—by doing, talking, and being busy, or by thinking about the past and worrying about the future. As Buddha has told us, there is only this moment.

Zhuang Zhou, the Chinese philosopher, said, "Tao is in the emptiness. Emptiness is the fast of the mind." Marcus Aurelius once wrote about "cutting free of impressions that cling to the mind, free of the future and the past," to become the "sphere rejoicing in its perfect stillness." Epictetus, Marcus's philosophical predecessor, said, "If we're anxious or nervous when we make the catch or throw, what will become of the game, and how can one maintain one's composure; how can one see what is coming next?"

Leaders make countless high-stakes decisions in the course of a day but only a minority find a couple of hours without chatter, without other people in their ear, where they can simply think (or not think), where they can recharge and find peace. Each of us needs to cultivate those moments in our lives when we limit distractions, noise and events so that we can access a deeper inner awareness of what's going on around us.

Solitude and social interaction are not either/or choices. Solitude is not the same as loneliness. Psychologists and therapists have often promoted the idea of a "time out" as a coping or replenishment strategy. Even then, the phrase "time out" suggests that, relating and stimulation are the important things in our lives and alone time merely a break or intermission. What if we viewed them as being equally important for our well-being?

Over the past 100 years we've had different perspectives on the concept of solitude. The word aloneness was coined in the medieval period signifying a completeness in one's singular being. In contrast, in religious terminology, solitude meant the experience of oneness with God. In our current world, most people believe being alone implies a lack of something. People who seek solitude are seen as anti-social or suffering from mental health issues.

To be sure, loneliness can be a debilitating and worrisome condition that can lead to mental health and behavioral problems. Loneliness can result from solitude. And loneliness can evoke childhood fears of abandonment and neglect.

Many societies that emphasize close-knit family patterns also provide structured and acceptable opportunities for solitude. For example, Western travellers to Japan in particular are impressed by the niches set aside in public spaces for individuals to sit alone, something that is viewed with respect and as a norm.

Being in touch with nature and solitude go hand-in-hand. The "tonic of wilderness," as Thoreau called it, is a theme that still resounds today. In 1993, Borge Ousland, a Norwegian explorer, made one of the most difficult treks in polar history. Pulling a 300-pound sled, he skied alone to the North Pole over more than 600 miles of drifting ice. Once or twice a week he communicated with his base camp by radio. After his extraordinary solo trek of 52 days, he said, "I had feared I would be lonely; I had never spent so much as a single night alone in a tent before... But being alone proved to be one of the greatest experiences of the entire trek."

William Deresiewicz writes about the value of solitude as a way for leaders to develop character and strengthening the mind. He says, how can leaders know the best thing to do in any situation "unless you've taken counsel with yourself in solitude? It seems to me that solitude is the very essence of leadership. The position of the leader is ultimately an intensely solitary, even intensely lonely one. How ever many people you may consult, you are the one who has to make the hard decisions. And at such moments, all you really have is yourself."

In my article, "Why Leaders Need Quiet Solitude," in Medium.com, I contend "Leaders have learned (and others expect it of them) to equate busyness and hurry--with the accompanying addictive adrenaline high--with a productive and satisfying life. Leaders who want to spend time alone and in reflection by contrast are looked upon with suspicion— 'he must be lonely,' or 'there must be something wrong.'"

An emerging body of research by Susan Cain, Robert Caplan and Daniel Gilbert, among others, shows that spending time alone is actually good for you and can contribute to a healthy mental, creative and emotional state.

Time alone can help us order our priorities based on our personal needs, not just what others want from us. "The paradigm experience of solitude is a state characterized by disengagement from the immediate demands of other people–a state of reduced social inhibition and increased freedom to select one's mental and physical activities," write researchers Christopher Long and James Averill. And neuroscientists would argue that when you can clear mental space in your brain's executive functional area, your cognitive and creative capacities improve.

According to Sherry Turkle, researcher and founder of the MIT Initiative on Technology and Self, it's important for people to intentionally set aside time each day when they abstain from activities like texting, tweeting, and Instagram – often the social junk food of choice for many of us. "The moment that people are alone, even for a few seconds, they become anxious, they panic, they fidget, they reach for a device. Just think of people at a checkout line or at a red light," Turkle says in her TED Talk "Connected, But Alone?" Turkle says that we should create sacred spaces where solitude is valued and embraced, and where we can—for an hour even at lunch at work—cut off distractions, particularly electronic devices.

Now, more than ever, we need our solitude. Aloneness can give us the power to regulate and adjust our lives. It can refill our energy well. Studies show that solitude is crucial for the development of the self. As authors James Averill and Christopher long highlighted in *Solitude: An Exploration of Benefits of Being Alone*, solitude is associated with freedom, creativity, intimacy, and spirituality.

In their book, *Lead Yourself: Inspiring Leadership Through Solitude*, authors Raymond M. Kethledge and Michael S. Erwin describe how solitude was a core feature in the lives of a number of famous influential and history making individuals including Abraham Lincoln, General Eisenhower, Jane Goodall, Winston Churchill, Martin Luther King Jr., and Pope John Paul II. They argue that solitude was a necessary practice in the development of their creativity, clarity of thought (both intuition and analysis), emotional balance and moral courage. The authors argue "leadership solitude is productive solitude, which means to use solitude purposely, with a particular end in mind. Productive solitude involves working your mind as you break down and sort and synthesize what is already there. When that process or work and isolation is successful, the result is an insight, or even a broader vision, that brings mind and soul together in clear-eyed, inspired conviction."

Mike Desjardins, Founder and CEO of Virtus Inc., a leadership development company based in Vancouver and a colleague of mine, described for me how reflection and solitude benefited him. He said "Through assessments, feedback, coaching, and mentoring, I became aware of how important my self-awareness was. The more I delved into my emotional intelligence, the more I realized how critical it was by my growth as a leader: if I wasn't self-aware then I couldn't empathize well with others, I wouldn't know I had been triggered, would end up in a default pattern that I couldn't self-regulate through, and then would feel bad about how I showed up in a situation afterwards. As well, when my motivation suffered, the more in-tune I was with my self-awareness, the better I could figure out how to get myself out of a funk."

I asked him about the issue of reflection time and solitude and he replied, "My mentor, Walt Sutton, said to me about ten years ago, 'if you want to take your leadership to the next level you need to do four things: build white space into your calendar, say no more often, start journaling, and make meditation a regular practice of at least 20-30 minutes.' I took his advice and put all of those things into place. I credit my even-temper, thoughtfulness, resilience, and stress-reduction to those habits. I have to say at the time I had no concept of how powerful those tools were going to be - they became game changers for me in my career and in my growth as a leader, husband, father, and friend."

Finally, I asked Mike what were the benefits he achieved. Mike replied, "Reduced stress, it's easier for me to stay present in conversation, I'm able to see the bigger picture more easily, I'm less triggered by situations, and I'm significantly more stoic in my approach to work and life (but it's definitely a journey that I'm on that I still have quite a way to go on). Now I crave more time for solitude and reflection which feels ironic in that I'm an extroverted person who loves to be with people. I didn't value the time and I used to think of it was 'dead space where I'm not productive,' while now I consider it the place where the real magic happens."

Specific Ways That Quiet Solitude Can Improve Self-Awareness

1. **Your brain actually grows.** A UCLA research study showed that regular times set aside to disengage, sit in silence, and mentally rest, improves the the "folding" of the cortex and boosts our ability to process information. A study published through the National Library of Medicine found that exposure to prolonged silence can actually cause the brain to produce new cells.

2. **Self-Awareness increases.** In silence, we can become more aware of our emotions and thoughts and engage in more detached reflection of them. The break from external stimuli can put us in tune to our inner voices. This enhanced awareness can lead to greater self-control. Silence brings our awareness back to the present.

3. **Memory improves.** Combining solitude with a walk in nature causes brain growth in the hippocampus region, resulting in better memory. Taking a walk alone gives the brain uninterrupted focus and helps with memory consolidation.

4. **Problem solving improves.** Our brains need to rest and recharge in order to function as well as we want them to. So even if you're not an introvert, alone time is still important

for processing and reflecting. "Constantly being on doesn't give your brain a chance to rest and replenish itself," Sherrie Bourg Carter, Psy.D. wrote in *Psychology Today*.

5. **Creativity is enhanced.** The creative process includes a crucial stage called incubation, where all the ideas we've been exposed to get to meet, mingle, marinate — then produce a eureka or "A-ha" moment. The secret to incubation? Doing nothing. What's typically seen as useless daydreaming is now being seen as an essential experience. Professor Jonathan Schooler from UC Santa Barbara says, "Daydreaming and boredom seem to be a source for incubation and creative discovery in the brain." When we're not focusing on anything in particular – instead letting the mind wander or dip into our deep storehouse of memories, ideas, and emotions – the brain's default mode network is activated. Many of our most original insights arise from the activity of this network.

6. **Relationships improve.** Solitude also enriches our connections with others by providing perspective, which enhances intimacy and fosters empathy. You think more critically about the role you play in others' lives and the role they play in yours. And when you do spend time with someone else, you're refreshed enough to really pay them due attention. After some calm, peaceful time on your own doing nothing, you can find things and people who irritate you reduce dramatically because you are now relaxed and more tolerant.

7. **You can become more mindful.** Elements of mindfulness such as being present, focusing your attention, emotional regulation and acceptance can be strengthened in aloneness and solitude, where you are free from distractions and

external stimuli. We need to balance between "doing" which is predominant in our culture and "being" which focuses on quiet reflection. In addition, strengthening our mindful practice of intentional responding rather than reacting by "autopilot" can be further enhanced.

8.   **Your physical health improves.** There is clear research evidence to demonstrate that regular periods of quiet solitude have benefits in heart and brain functioning as well as overall health.

Solitude has been a key to the effectiveness of leaders throughout history, but we are now in danger of losing the value of it without being aware. A leader must strike a balance between solitude and interaction with others, but the leaders today face enormous pressure to skew the balance toward interaction. Being alone, seeking solitude in preference to always being with others is now seen as a mental health issue, or behavioral dysfunction.

Some organizations are beginning to recognize that the pressure for constant relationships behaviors in the form of meetings, electronic communication, and open offices may actually be a cause for productivity and employee well-being problems, and have moved away from these practices to product employee work time, and provide places where employees can be in solitude and quiet.

17

How Reading Fiction Aids Self-Reflection

"Not all readers are leaders, but all leaders are readers."

President Harry S. Truman

One of the ways which can help leaders become more self-reflective and enhance self-awareness is to develop the habit of reading. A distinction must be made here. The positive effect is not as pronounced with non-fiction as it is with fiction.

When was the last time you read a good novel?

Reading fiction not only is a great recreational activity, it also slows cognitive decline. One study showed that older readers have a 32 % lower rate of mental decline compared to their peers who didn't read. In addition to slower memory decline, those who read more have been found to show fewer characteristics of Alzheimer's disease, according to a 2001 study published in the journal *Proceedings of the National Academy of Sciences*. According to neuroscientist Daniel Levitin, focused reading uses about 42 calories per hour, whereas absorbing new information (e.g., scanning Twitter or the news headlines) burns around 65 calories per hour.

Research has found that reading novels improves our brain functions on a variety of levels, including the ability to put yourself in another person's shoes and flex your imagination. It also boosts our innovative thinking skills. Take it from Elon Musk, arguably one of the most innovative minds of our time. He's said that growing up, he spent more than 10 hours a day pouring through science fiction novels. In today's rapidly changing world, innovation is necessary for any business to stay competitive.

What Are Some Other Benefits?

Reading fiction enhances creativity. Fiction often presents mystery uncertainty. In the movies, we often long for an anticipated if not certain happy ending. But fiction can be much more ambiguous. In that way, fiction enhances creativity. A study published in *Creativity Research Journal* asked students to read either a short fictional story or a non-fiction essay and then measured their emotional need for certainty and stability. Researchers discovered that the fiction readers had less need for "cognitive closure" than those who read non-fiction, and added: "These findings suggest that reading fictional literature could lead to better procedures of processing information generally, including those of creativity."

Reading fiction can extend your life. Researcher Avi Bivishi and colleagues, writing in the journal *Social Science and Medicine*, reported reading a book for 30 minutes every day forecasts a sharper, healthier mind, which predicted a 20% lower odds of dying about a decade later.

Neuroscientists have discovered that reading a novel can improve brain function on a variety of levels. The recent study on the brain benefits of reading fiction was conducted at Emory

University. The study titled, "Short- and Long-Term Effects of a Novel on Connectivity in the Brain," was recently published in the journal *Brain Connectivity*. The researchers found that becoming engrossed in a novel enhances connectivity in the brain and improves brain function.

Reading Stories helps you become more inclusive, tolerant and open-minded. A study published in the *Journal of Applied Social Psychology*, had tested whether the novels of Harry Potter could be used for improving tolerance. After three experiments in which students read passages of the books about discrimination, the students showed changed attitudes about everything from immigrants to gay students. The researchers concluded that young children, with the help of a teacher, "were able to understand that Harry's frequent support of 'mudbloods' was an allegory towards bigotry in real-life society." Also, in a 2019 study, researchers found that reading fiction modestly improved people's capacity to understand and mentally react to other individuals and social situations, and by and large, that was after reading a single story.

Reading fiction makes you happier. A survey of 1,500 adult readers in the UK found that 76% of them said reading improves their life and helps to make them feel good. Other finds of the survey are that those who read books regularly are on average more satisfied with life, happier, and more likely to feel that the things they do in life are worthwhile.

Reading fiction makes you more likely to help others. A study by D.R. Johnson and colleagues, published in the *Psychology of Aesthetics, Creativity, and the Arts*, found those people who regularly read fiction were more likely to be prosocial and help others in need.

Reading fiction helps you be less biased toward other cultures and races. A study by Dan R. Johnson and colleagues, published *Basic and Social Psychology*, concluded that those people who regularly read fiction about other cultures and ethnic groups lessened their racial stereotypes and biases.

The Value of "Deep Reading"

Research has identified something called "deep reading," which is slow, immersive and reflective. It is in sharp contrast to superficial reading, such as what we do via social media platforms or emails and texting, which is quick and non-reflective.

Deep reading lends itself to fiction. The structure of the printed page is uniquely conducive to the deep reading experience. A book's lack of hyperlinks, for example, frees the reader from making decisions — should I click on this link or not? — allowing the reader to remain fully immersed in the narrative.

The immersion fostered by deep reading is supported by the way the brain handles language rich in detail, allusion and metaphor: By creating a mental representation that draws on the same brain regions that would be active if the scene were unfolding in real life. The emotional situations and moral dilemmas in fictional stories put us inside the minds of fictional characters and even, as studies suggest, increases our real-life capacity for open-mindedness, empathy and compassion.

The deep reader, protected from distractions and attuned to the nuances of language, enters a state that psychologist Victor Nell, in his study of the psychology of pleasure reading, likens to a hypnotic trance. Nell found that when readers are enjoying the experience the most, the pace of their reading actually slows. The combination of fast, fluent decoding of words and slow, unhurried progress on the page gives deep readers time to enrich their reading with reflection, analysis, and their own memories and opinions.

Leaders should regularly read novels as a way of strengthening their leadership skills. I recommend to my executive coaching leader clients that they undertake, if they have not done so already, regularly reading fiction as a way of improving well-being, learning how to slow down, understand others, and reduce stress.

18

The Self-Awareness Scorecard for Robert and Daniel

"By becoming self-aware, you gain ownership of reality; in becoming real, you become the master of both inner and outer life."

Deepak Chopra

How did Robert and Daniel, our case studies first outlined at the beginning of this book, fare, given the foregoing analysis and research on self-awareness? The following chart provides a detailed description on how Robert and Daniel performed on each element of self-awareness as described in the book.

A Comparison of Robert's and Daniel's Self-Awareness

Element	Robert	Daniel
Regular times for self-reflection	Robert rarely scheduled time for regular self-reflection.	Daniel scheduled 30 minutes of self-reflection per week. He also took time to briefly reflect both before and after meetings.
Purpose in life	Robert's focus in life was largely external and transactional. He never reflected on what his greater purpose was beyond his job.	Daniel engaged in a formal process of identifying his personal purpose in life beyond the definition of his work.

Clarification and reaffirmation of personal values	Robert clarified his values once as part of workshop he attended when he was first appointed as CEO, but did not engage in regular review.	Daniel clarified and annually reaffirmed his personal values, and compared them with his organization's values in a formal process with his coach.
Self-efficacy	Robert was very self-confident, and was seen by many as being arrogant, yet the confidence in his abilities was not matched by others' perception of him, nor were his actual successes.	Daniel had a quiet confidence about him, which never manifested as a "know-it-all" arrogant attitude. But he knew what he was capable of, and didn't hesitate to ask for help or admit what he didn't know or couldn't do.

Emotional self-regulation and triggers	Robert all too frequently in meetings and conversations would react with anger or rudeness when his authority or ideas were challenged.	Daniel had a reputation of being calm and measured in his conversations and team meetings, even when facing a crisis or upsetting event. That seemed to spread to his team in beneficial ways.
Blind spots and biases	Robert was unaware (not ignorant) of his blind spots, as often illustrated by his confirmation biases, and close mindedness to new or challenging ideas.	Daniel had engaged in a serious manner a self-awareness assessment, which included identifying blind spots, and had modified his behavior as a result.
Strengths and weaknesses	Robert did not complete a strengths and weaknesses assessment or 360-degree assessment.	Daniel took his 360-degree feedback seriously, and created an individual development plan to address those weaknesses.

Self-deception	Robert had a number of blind spots and biases which prevented him from seeing reality, or others' perspectives. As a result, he had deceived himself as to the way reality was. He had little interest in discovering those blind spots nor did he think it was that important compared to how he believed he was "right."	Daniel had engaged in a 360-degree assessment which showed others' perceptions. In addition, in his coaching sessions, we identified his blind spots and biases, and what he might want to do about them.
Emotional Intelligence	Robert completed an emotional intelligence assessment which showed significant concerns, and which identified a	Daniel scored high on the emotional intelligence assessment, which was reaffirmed in his 360 feedback from his team. He also scored well on an EQ assessment.

	lack of self-awareness, compassion and empathy as significant issues, but he did not develop plans to address those issues.	
Core Beliefs	Robert appeared to not have any strong beliefs about anything, but saw each event and interchange with people from a transactional perspective-- "how can I win," and "what's in it for me," and "the ends justifies the means."	Daniel had strong core beliefs about basic values in life such as honesty, compassion, service. In addition, he had developed a personal code related to character traits which governed his interactions with people (e.g.: integrity).

Perspective on internal vs. external world	Because of his reticence for engaging in self-awareness and self-reflection, Robert rarely reflected on his internal emotional state, nor the impact he was having on others.	Daniel had developed mindfulness practices around both acceptance of his emotions, labelling those emotions when they occurred which aided in self-regulation; and he was keenly aware of how his actions and behaviors impacted others' emotional states.
Mind wandering	In meetings and conversations, Robert would frequently check his phone for messages, or be thinking about his next meeting or issue. Others commented on him "not paying attention" to discussion in meetings. He was constantly engaged in multitasking.	In his mindfulness training, Daniel had practiced and enhanced his capacity for focused attention, and removing distractions. His mind wandering was limited to self-initiated quiet times for creative reflection.

Focus on "ups and downs" of external world	Robert frequently saw and experienced life as a "roller-coaster" ride, feeling elated when things were "up", and prone to frustration and anger when things were "down."	Daniel accepted that a natural part of life included "ups and downs", and did not excessively react to either, but instead he developed and practiced equanimity.
Resilience	Robert's resilience was limited, partly due to his belief that there should be no "downs" or untoward events in life that could not be forcibly removed. As a result, he would "flail" with frustration in the "down" periods.	Daniel had a strong capacity for "bouncing back" from negative events or unfavorable results, not dwelling on the past.

Self-identity	Robert's view of his identity was the persona he wanted to project— confident, decisive, dominating. He did not spend time reflecting on his inner self and who he wanted to be.	Daniel had an impressive clarity about who he was, and it aligned with how others saw him. He consistently acted in alignment with his values, his sense of purpose and his actions reflected that.
Solitude and Stillness	To my knowledge, Robert did not spend time alone in solitude to be still and reflect. He was always with other people, or engaged in activities.	Daniel, on a quarterly basis, would take a solitary retreat to his family cabin in the woods. Every day he would, after working, take a solitary walk to gather his thoughts and reflect, with no goal or planned activity.

Mindfulness	My impression was that Robert often was not aware of the emotions he was feeling, partly because of his reactive nature, and when asked, he had trouble with labelling his emotions. Also, due to his multitasking and inability to hold his attention and focus in the present moment, he always appeared "busy" and harried.	Daniel had taken up mindfulness meditation early in his life, and was a seasoned practitioner. He was clearly able to beware of his inner thoughts and feelings as they occurred, capable of pausing before responding to events and people. He also had an impressive capacity for focusing in the moment on whatever he was doing, or on what others were saying.

Reading Fiction	Robert's reading was restricted to non-fiction business books, and even there, mostly business summaries or audio books. He did not read fiction.	Daniel was a prolific reader of at least 2 books per week, mostly works of fiction and biographies.
Self-Awareness Assessment (self and 360)	To my knowledge Robert did not engage in any formal self-awareness assessment and his Board did not insist on a 360.recommended that he complete the EQi assessment but he did not agree to do so.	Daniel had completed an EQi assessment and debriefed it with me, as well as a 360 assessment which we also debriefed. And he reviewed them with his Board.

Slowing Down	Robert's demeanor reflected "busyness" and he was often late to meetings. He seemed incapable of slowing down. He saw slowing down as a weakness.	In addition to valuing and engaging in solitude retreats and reflection time, Daniel had an intuitive understanding when it was time to slow down and reflect, and not be in a hurried mode of operating.

19

The Self-Aware Leader

*"At the center of your being
you have the answer;
you know who you are
and you know what you want."*
Lao Tzu

Self-aware leaders possess the qualities that progressive organizations look for. The competency that organizations look for in leaders is the ability of an individual to perceive one's own attitudes and personality, strengths and weakness, values and desires, abilities and deficiencies, and goals. Authentic leaders are those who are cognizant of their own existence, self-resources and the context in which they operate. Self-awareness can generate greater authenticity, which can in turn, lead to greater self-regulation.

In an article in *Harvard Business Review*, Tasha Eurich argues "Across the studies we examined, two broad categories of self-awareness kept emerging. The first, which we dubbed internal self-awareness, represents how clearly we see our own values, passions, aspirations fit with our environment, reactions (including thoughts, feelings, behaviors, strengths, and weaknesses), and impact on others. We've found that internal self-awareness is associated with higher job and relationship satisfaction, personal and social control, and happiness; it is negatively related to anxiety, stress, and depression."

She adds, "The second category, external self-awareness, means understanding how other people view us, in terms of those same factors listed above. Our research shows that people who know how others see them are more skilled at showing empathy and taking others' perspectives. For leaders who see themselves as their employees do, their employees tend to have a better relationship with them, feel more satisfied with them, and see them as more effective in general."

In 2008, Kevin Cashman published *Leadership from the Inside Out*, a breakthrough bestseller, in which he described how inner mastery leads to great leadership. Since its publication, the book has been integrated into the curricula of more than 100 universities, and its concepts have influenced numerous leadership programs. Other subsequent research has validated many of Cashman's leadership principles.

Cashman provides a critique about how we have traditionally viewed leadership as an external event focusing on what the leader does, rather than who the leader is. He argues the two are totally inseparable. He argues that western society's training, development and educational systems focus on learning about what to think, rather than how to think; what to do, rather than how to be; and what to achieve, rather than how to achieve. People learn about things, not the nature of things, filling up on knowledge but rarely understanding the importance of comprehending knowledge, expanding it, or using it more effectively, he says.

Leadership, Cashman argues, is not something people simply do but comes from a deeper reality within an individual's values, principles, life experiences, and essence. He says good leadership is an intimate expression of what the individual is--the whole person in action.

Cashman believes that when people define their identities and purpose only in terms of external truths, the circumstances of their lives define them. In this externally driven state of identity, life is fragile, vulnerable, and at risk, and core identities and passionate purposes are overshadowed by life's events. For individuals in this state, success may even be present, but mastery escapes them. Without knowing it, they choose to "major" in the "minor" things of life. Thus, they are unable to lead because they fail to see beyond the external circumstances surrounding them.

Cashman calls the inward journey the experience of "Being Purpose" that connects silence to leadership: "With no silence, there is no reflection. With no reflection, there is no vision. With no vision, there is no leadership... silence and reflection are actually performance pathways to more expanded vision and more effective, innovative leadership."

The human species has a unique capacity to contemplate not only their present state, but also their ideal state, imagining a future that is better than the past. Intertwined are processes of self-reflexive thought, self-examination, and introspection. Self-awareness enables one to focus attention inward and study oneself.

We can look to historical reasons for the absence of self-awareness. Researchers Mark Leary and Nicole Buttermore argue in an article, "Levels of Networked Self-Awareness," that our capacity for self-reflection may account for the rapid appearance of human civilization 40,000 - 60,000 years ago." They attribute the rapid growth in human civilization during this time to the capacity to think symbolically and abstractly about ourselves.

Some researchers have defined self-awareness as simply the degree to which our view of ourselves matches that of others. Leaders whose self-ratings of performance are congruent with performance ratings by others, can be seen as having high levels of self-awareness. Using this standard, researchers Greg Ashley and Roni Reiter-Palmon concluded that a large body of empirical research has accrued suggesting those leaders with high levels of self-awareness tend to have better performance outcomes than those with lower levels of self-awareness. Moreover, they found congruence between subordinates' evaluation of their leaders and the leaders' self- evaluation may lead to increased levels of subordinate work satisfaction.

According to researcher Anthony Gatling and his colleagues, leaders can increase their self-awareness by:

- understanding psychological strengths and emotional triggers.
- recognizing how dark side personality traits such as the need for approval, tendency to be judgmental, and the need for perfection and control adversely affect relationships.
- identifying feelings and emotions (e.g. frustration, vulnerability, elation) and the role these play in both easy and difficult interactions.

Patricia Ann Castelli, writing in the *Journal of Management Development.* argues "Leaders must challenge the status quo and become reflective by seeking universal truths and listening to their inner, intuitive voice. Current social and economic changes call for a more reflective style of leadership that will integrate human potential rather than splinter it. Internal characteristics such as critical thinking, long-term planning and finding innovative ways to solve problems with an equal focus on people and profit is the basis for reflective leadership."

Leaders who formally conduct such a moral self-assessment are more likely to honor those criteria and lead with greater integrity. By emphasizing the importance of examining their moral standards and understanding their personal motivation to lead, leaders will not only increase their self-awareness but improve their ability to explain the justification for moral decisions.

Research in 2013 by Korn Ferry analysts David Zes and Dana Landis shows the connection between self-awareness and organizational financial performance. In their white paper, entitled "A Better Return on Self-Awareness," an analysis of the stock performance of 486 companies and administering 6,977 self-assessments to the professionals within those companies, they concluded "public companies with a higher rate of return (ROR) also employ professionals who exhibit higher levels of self-awareness." In addition, their research found employees at poor-performing companies had 20% more blind spots than better financially performing companies and employees at poor-performing companies were 79% more likely to have low self-awareness than those at firms with robust ROR.

In another study by Korn Ferry they found that 92% of leaders skilled at the Emotional Self-Awareness competency had high energy and high performance teams. In contrast, leaders with low self-awareness created negative workplace climates.

A study conducted in 2010 by Green Peak Partners and Cornell's School of Industrial and Labor Relations of 72 executives at public and private companies. They all had revenues from $50 million to $5 billion, and it was found that "a high self-awareness score was the strongest predictor of overall success."

Authentic leaders are motivated to seek accurate and balanced assessments regarding themselves and their performance, and to act on these assessments. Authenticity, which implies being true to and aware of one's self and others, is enhanced by leveraging moments of intentional awareness and reflection to shape one's leadership competence and that of others.

Self-Awareness and Transformational Leadership

Originally developed by leadership expert Bernard Bass, transformational leadership is conceptualized as a method of motivating and inspiring followers through the articulation of a compelling vision. It encompasses behaviors such as considering individuals' needs, effective role modelling of values and ideals, as well as stimulating and challenging followers to think differently. Transformational leaders aim to help to motivate followers through intrinsic rewards, not exclusively through extrinsic rewards. Research has further identified that heightened levels of self-awareness are related to four components of transformational leadership: inspirational motivation, intellectual stimulation, individual consideration, and idealized influence.

Various research studies have shown how leader self-awareness has a positive impact on follower motivation, as well as employees' feelings of cohesiveness, commitment and performance. The association between levels of self-awareness and perceived transformational leadership behaviors is apparent within the research.

In a study where levels of leader self-awareness were measured by both the leader and followers within an IT company, results showed that more self-aware leaders demonstrated heightened levels of transformational leadership behaviors. The study also found there was a positive association between self-aware leaders and followers' levels of satisfaction.

Recent research has found that team performance and individual worker productivity can be significantly enhanced through greater self-awareness:

- Researcher Joyce Ehrlinger and her colleagues found that team members with low self-awareness had more difficulty managing work relationships and contribute well as a team member.
- David Whiteside and Laurie Barclay concluded, based on their research, that self-awareness as a means to promote fairness among managers with low empathy was a powerful strategy.
- A study by the Cornell University Center for Advanced Human Resource Studies found the level of an individual team member's self-awareness affected the overall team's self-awareness and subsequently the team's performance.
- A study by Erich C. Dierdorff and Robert S. Rubin found in a 2014 meta-analysis of 357,000 workers that overall they were poor judges of their own capabilities; there was a large gap in workers' self-assessments and those of their team members; teams with less self-aware individuals made worse

decisions, engaged in less coordination and showed less conflict management skills.

- In another study published in the *Journal of Management*, the researchers analyzed the performance of 515 teams comprised of 2700 individuals, and found that when teams have members with lower levels of self-awareness, team coordination and cohesion suffered.

In the case of leaders and team members, multiple self-awareness strategies can be developed and used effectively to raise their self-awareness, and these should be incorporated into and be a centerpiece to leadership development and training programs.

In a research study, Paul McDonald at the University of Wellington's School of Management, argues the following:

"Self-awareness is gained through introspection and personal insight and externally through social interaction and attention to one's social impact. It is an awareness and trust in one's motives, feelings and desires and self-relevant cognitions." He goes on to say, "It is important for leaders to avoid denial, distortion and or exaggeration and remain objective, and therefore ego defence mechanisms may compel individuals to engage in self-delusion both in terms of private self-knowledge and externally based evaluative information."

A 2012 survey of 75 members of the Stanford Graduate School of Business Advisory Council rated self-awareness as the most important capability for leaders to develop. In an article in *Fortune International*, Lauren Zalaznick, now chairman of Entertainment & Digital Networks and Integrated Media for NBC-Universal, recalled that the best advice she ever received was from her first boss, who told her: "Throughout your career, you're going to hear lots of feedback from show makers and peers and employees and bosses. If you hear a certain piece of feedback consistently and you don't agree with it, it doesn't matter what you think. Truth is, you're being perceived that way."

But some executives resist this process for a long time. Take the case of David Pottruck, the former CEO of Charles Schwab. Earlier in his career, he was summoned to his boss's office and told that his colleagues did not trust him. As Pottruck recalled in the *Harvard Business Review*, "That feedback was like a dagger to my heart. I was in denial, as I didn't see myself as others saw me. ... I had no idea how self-serving I looked to other people. Still, somewhere in my inner core the feedback resonated as true."

It's clear from the research on leadership effectiveness that self-awareness can be one of most reliable and desirable traits of a leader than separates poor or even dysfunctional leaders from the best ones.

With respect to the hundreds of leaders that I had the opportunity to train, coach or mentor over a thirty-year period, I found that accurate and elevated self-awareness was the most salient factor in the success or failure of those leaders. With respect to our two case studies, Robert and Daniel, it is clear that Robert was an unaware leader, who had extreme difficulty both accessing his own internal emotional state and being aware of the perceptions others had of him, and took little or no time for reflection before and after acting. In contrast, Daniel was a thoughtful and reflective leader who had recognized the value and need for greater self-awareness.

20

Strategies for Developing Your Self-Awareness

"Without self-awareness we are as babies in the cradles."

Virginia Woolf

Here are some ways in which leaders (and the general public also) can enhance and develop their self-awareness and self-reflection. For a detailed list of the kinds of questions leaders can ask themselves to raise awareness see Appendix A. To complete a Self-Awareness Assessment, see Appendix B.

Set aside regular and structured time for self-reflection (daily or weekly). "Calendarize" it just as you would a meeting or appointment. Some self-aware executives I know do this on a Monday morning or on Sunday evening to set up a positive mindset for the week.

Become the observer of your mind through mindfulness meditation. Keep your attention focused on your breath. If you notice your mind wandering to other thoughts, gently return your attention to your breath.

159

Talk to yourself from a detached perspective. There's a voice inside your head, sometimes two. It's your internal dialogue or commentary that tries to help you make decisions, although sometimes this voice can be your critic Gremlin. Instead of engaging with this voice by arguing or blocking it, become the observer of your voice from a detached perspective. From this detached perspective, you can resist passing judgment about your thoughts as being either good or bad, but rather seeing them as "just as they are."

Pay attention to what bothers you about other people and that become emotional "triggers." Often the things that irritate us the most in other people are a reflection of some quality we dislike in ourselves. So, whenever someone does something that seems to particularly annoy or irritate you, ask yourself: *Could this be a reflection of something in me that I dislike? Do I do some version of that?*

Label your thoughts and emotions. When you are feeling strong negative emotions or thoughts, pause and observe them. Self-mastery requires this observation and recognition. Label the emotions and thoughts without judgment and with acceptance. What's important is how you act upon those thoughts or emotions, not whether you are experiencing them.

Play "devil's advocate." Challenging your thought patterns and reasoning will help with self-mastery. Putting on the other shoe and playing devil's advocate will uncover weaknesses and holes in your thinking. Challenging the veracity of your thoughts will result in making better decisions. You'll be able to iron out any unreasonable biases that appear in your logic. Whatever decision you're working through, come at it from as many different angles as possible. Debate with yourself, have a spirited argument. You may be surprised at some of the insights you come up with.

Develop a belief that there are not good and bad emotions, there are only good and bad behaviors. All emotions serve a purpose, and learning to accept how you are feeling at the time is healthy. We don't want to feel angry, fearful, anxious, or ashamed. And while we all recoil from negative emotions, each of us tends to have one particular negative emotion that we especially dislike and try to avoid. By avoiding the emotion, we're avoiding listening to what the emotion has to say to us. Negative emotions are painful because our mind is trying to get our attention, sometimes for a very good reason. Learning to tolerate the discomfort of our negative emotions can unlock a wealth of insight about ourselves and our world if we're willing to listen.

Learn to recognize "cognitive distortions," and biases. These are inaccurate thoughts and beliefs that warp how we see things, including ourselves, and biases that affect our beliefs. Examples are confirmation bias, catastrophizing, blaming. Catch yourself when you notice you've lapsed into that kind of thinking.

Keep A Journal. The more you journal, the more you are aware of your behaviors and thought patterns, and subsequently, the more ability you have to change and grow. Writing not only helps us process our thoughts but also makes us feel connected and at peace with ourselves. Research shows that recording things we are grateful for or our challenges helps increase happiness and satisfaction.

Travel and learn about other cultures, to gain different perspectives. Spending all your time with your "tribe," geographic location or cultural influences can increasingly narrow your perspective. Find our how other people see things, so you can reflect on your own perceptions.

Conduct a cognitive reappraisal. This psychological strategy can be understood in the question, *Is the glass half empty or half full?* Cognitive reappraisal is reinterpreting or reframing a negative event in a way that reduces the negative response or completely replaces it with a positive one.

Turn off your autopilot. Identify one of your automatic behaviors or habits that you are unhappy about or would like to change and commit to changing it.

State or reaffirm your values. Write down your most important values and ideals associated with your personal life and work and imagine ways that you can ensure they are in alignment with your behaviors.

State, clarify and reaffirm your core beliefs, and how they relate to your identity. What we believe about ourselves, others and the world help to shape our identity and how we present that identity to the world.

Recognize and deal with your inner conflicts. Resolve any beliefs, values or emotions that you may have that are in conflict with each other.

Read high quality fiction. The very best writers are expert observers of human nature in particular. It's their job to notice the tiny details of thought, emotion, desire, and action that most of us miss amid the frantic business of daily life. And even though most of us probably aren't called to be authors and astute observers of human nature professionally, we can all learn a thing or two about ourselves by learning to pay attention like an author. By describing people carefully, good fiction teaches us how to think about people carefully and with compassion. And the better we get at observing others, the more likely we are to look at ourselves the same way.

Do a Self-Awareness Assessment. See Appendix B.

Ask yourself some self-awareness questions and write your answers in a journal. Periodically review them. See Appendix A.

Work with a formal mentor, coach or counsellor. They can provide skilful feedback and issues for self-examination that will assist you greatly toward self-mastery.

Draw a timeline of your life. Spend 20 minutes drawing a timeline of your life starting with your birth, and mark the major events in your life along the timeline. Specifically, note events that had an impact on you--big or small, positive or negative. This helps you to make sense of or get a new perspective on an especially distressing or difficult time by seeing that specific period "in context."

Ask for feedback from others (and take it well), independent of any formal assessment. Most people don't deliberately seek feedback about themselves from others, unless it's as a result of a process at work. There are many aspects of ourselves that we can see need improvement, it's the parts of ourselves we can't see--our blind spots--that are the real problem. And other people are uniquely positioned to notice these and help us see them.

Be a better listener and observer. Practice being a better listener for others, by consistently practicing your active listening skills. This can include restraining your impulse to think about your response while they are speaking. Good listening should not only involve your cognitive processes, but also something called "empathetic listening," which is noticing the feelings and emotions being expressed by the speaker. Finally, spend less time speaking, and more time listening (70-30 is good), which facilitates your ability to notice more about what's going on.

Allocate "do nothing" time in your schedule. Research has shown that regular periods of time in which you are not engaging in "doing" or tasks enhances your productivity, well-being and creativity.

Be rigorous about screening distractions in your life. Constantly being interrupted by a cell-phone, email, TV or meetings has been shown to negatively impact our cognitive performance and increase stress. Also, most of these distractions are in the "external" world, and have no connection to our inner state, and therefore can actually mask, not enhance our self-awareness.

Regularly seek out time for solitude silence and stillness. This engages your mind in a different, creative and productive way, and gives you the opportunity to reflect without interruptions, or be engaged in activities. It also has been proven to enhance physical well-being.

Learn and regularly practice mindfulness meditation. This activity has been shown to aid in cognitive focus and attention, as well as enhancing non-judgment, acceptance and compassion.

Recognize your "inner parents." How are you a reflection of your parents? The influence of our parents is pervasive. Beliefs, values, behaviors and personal paradigms are all heavily influenced by our parents. How are you carrying your parental influence?

Reflect and take action on how you may engage in self-sabotage. Getting in our own way or creating our own obstacles can prevent you form fully engaging in self-awareness. Do you know how you sabotage your efforts or behaviors? Are you blaming others instead of looking inwards? What are you doing about it?

Afterword

"To see a World in a Grain of Sand
And a Heaven in a Wild Flower,
Hold Infinity in the palm of your hand
And Eternity in an hour."

William Blake

For the past 40 years, I have been actively involved with organizations--large and small--in the public and private sectors as a high school principal, Superintendent of Schools, CEO, senior executive, management consultant, teacher and trainer and with my own executive coaching company. This experience has afforded me the privilege and challenge of being a leader, and mentoring and coaching experienced and new leaders.

I have worked with hundreds of executives, professionals and entrepreneurs to help them achieve their goals, be happier in their lives, have better relationships and learn how to overcome obstacles to achieve what they want. Over the years I've seen numerous executive careers derailed by lack of self-awareness. Individuals felt they were omnipotent or took crazy risks or didn't recognize when actions they felt were "brilliant" were actually demoralizing for others, or in general didn't have an accurate "read" on how others were decoding the messages they were sending.

On the other hand, the most effective executives I knew had, I believe, realistic assessments of their own abilities—their strengths and weaknesses, their effect on others. In the process of working with them, it was clear to me that a central overriding theme was the degree to which they were self-aware, and if they took time to deliberately reflect on themselves and their lives.

So many people now, leaders among them, focus on the external world as both causes and solutions to the problems we face. And most assuredly, problems such as climate change, income inequality, poverty, violence and war can present themselves to be external to our inner state. Yet we increasingly resort to defining the importance and value of the world in those external terms--the things we own, the profit and loss statements, the cars we drive and technology we invent. But as the ancients have told us for centuries, the real quality of our lives, the essence of who were are, is to be found within ourselves. Without rejecting the external world, we can bring a better balance to it by being more in touch with our inner selves and the impact that awareness has on our actions and relationships.

References

Ackerman, L. (2005). *The Identity Code: The 8 Essential Questions for Finding Your Purpose and Place in the World.* New York: Random House.

Argandoña, A. (2015). Humility in management. *Journal of Business Ethics* 132, 63–71.

Akinola, M. (2010). Measuring the pulse of an organization: Integrating physiological measures into the organizational scholar's toolbox. *Research in Organizational Behavior*, 30, 203-223.

Albert, S. and Whetten, D.A. (1985). Organizational identity. In L. L. Cummings and M. M. Staw (Eds.), *Research in Organizational Behavior*, Vol. 7. pp. 263–295. Greenwich, CT: JAI Press.

Altman, D. (2010). *The Mindfulness Code: Keys for Overcoming Stress, Anxiety, Fear, and Unhappiness.* Novato, CA: New World Library.

Anderson, A.K. (2007). Attending to the present: mindfulness meditation reveals distinct neural modes of self-reference. *Scan*, 2, 313–322.

Aquino, K. and Reed, A.II. (2002). The self-importance of moral identity. *Journal of Personality and Social Psychology*, 83 (6), 1423–1440.

Argandona, A. (2015). Humility in management. *Journal of Business Ethics*, 132 (1), 63-71.

Ardelt, M., and Grunwald, S. (2018). The importance of self-reflection and awareness for human development in hard times. *Research in Human Development*, 15, 187-199.

Ashforth, B. E., Harrison, S. H., & Corley, K. G. (2008). Identification in organizations: An examination of four fundamental questions. *Journal of Management*, 34, 325-374.

Ashforth, B. E., & Mael, F. (1989). Social identity theory and the organization. *Academy of Management Review*, 14, 20-39.

Atkins, P. W. B., Styles R., Atkins P.W.B., & Styles R. (2015). *Mindfulness, Identity and Work: Mindfulness Training Creates a More Flexible Sense of Self. Mindfulness in Organizations: Foundations, Research, and Applications.* Cambridge: Cambridge University Press.

Ashford, S. J. (1989). Self-Assessments in organizations, a literature review and integrative model. *Research in Organizational Behavior*, 11, 133–174.

Ashford, S. J. (1986), Feedback-Seeking in individual adaptation: A resource Perspective, *Academy of Management Journal*, 29, 465-487.

Ashford, S. J. & Tsui, A.S. (1991), Self-regulation for managerial effectiveness: The role of active feedback seeking. *Academy of Management Journal*, 34, 251-280.

Atwater, L. E., Ostroff, C., Yammarino, F. J., & Fleenor, J. W. (1998). Self-other agreement: Does it really matter? *Personnel Psychology*, 51, 577-598.

Austin, J. H. (2006). *Zen-Brain Reflections*. Cambridge, MA: MIT Press.

Avolio, B.J., & Gardner, W.L. (2005). Authentic leadership: Getting to the root of positive forms of leadership. *The Leadership Quarterly*, 16, 315–338.

Avolio, B. J., Gardner, W. L., Walumbwa, F. O., Luthans, F., & May,D. R. (2004). Unlocking the mask: A look at the process by which authentic leaders impact follower attitudes and behaviors. *The Leadership Quarterly*, 15, 801–823.

Avolio, A.J. et al. (2009). A meta-analytic review of leadership impact research: Experimental and quasi-experimental studies. *The Leadership Quarterly*, 20, 764–784.

Ayduk, O., & Kross, E. (2010). From a distance: implications of spontaneous self-distancing for adaptive self-reflection. *Journal of Personality and Social Psychology*, 98, 809–829.

Bal, P. M., & Veltkamp, M. (2013). How does fiction reading influence empathy? An experimental investigation on the role of emotional transportation. *PLoS One*, 8 (1), 55-63.

Baumeister, R.F., Vohs, K.D. and Tice, D.M. (2003). The strength model of self-control. *Current Directions in Psychological Science*, 16 (6), 351-355.

Baumeister, R. F., & Vohs, K. D. (2003). Self-regulation and the executive function of the self. In M. R. Leary & J. P. Tangney (Eds.), *Handbook of Self and Identity* (pp. 197–217). New York: Guildford Press.

Baumeister, R. F., Smart L., & Boden J. M. (1996). Relation of threatened egotism to violence and aggression: the dark side of high self-esteem. *Psychology Review*, 103, 5–33.

Bass, B. (1985). *Leadership and Performance Beyond Expectations*. New York: Collier Macmillan.

Boyatzis, R. E. & Akrivou, K. (2006). The ideal self as the driver of intentional change. *Journal of Management Development*, 25 (7), 624–642.

Boyatzis, R. E. & McKee A. (2005). *Resonant Leadership*. Boston, MA: Harvard Business School.

Brewer, M. B. & Gardner, W. (1996) Who is this "we?" Levels of collective identity and self-representations. *Journal of Personality and Social Psychology*, 71, 83–93.

Brower, P. J. (1964). The power to see ourselves. *Harvard Business Review*, 42, 156–165.

Burke, P. J. & D. C. Reitzes. (1981). The link between identity and role performance. *Social Psychology Quarterly*, 44 (2), 83–92.

Barling, J., Slater, F., & Kevin Kelloway, E. (2000). Transformational leadership and emotional intelligence: An exploratory study. *Leadership & Organization Development Journal*, 21 (3), 157-161.

Baer, R.A., Smith, G.T., Lykins, E., Button, D., Krietemeyer, J., Sauer, S. & Williams, J.M.G. (2008). Construct validity of the Five Facet Mindfulness Meditation Questionnaire in meditating and non-meditating samples. *Assessment*, 15 (3), 329-342.

Bavishi, A., Slade, M.D., & Levy, B.R. (2016). A chapter a day: Association of book reading with longevity. *Social Science and Medicine*, 164, 44-48.

Brendel, W., Hankerson, S., Byun, S. & Cunningham, B. (2016). Cultivating leadership Dharma: Measuring the impact of regular mindfulness meditation practice on creativity, resilience, tolerance for ambiguity, anxiety and stress. *Journal of Management Development*, 35 (8), 1056-1078.

Brown, K.W. & Ryan, R.M. (2003), The benefits of being present: Mindfulness meditation and its role in psychological well-being. *Journal of Personality and Social Psychology*, 84 (4), 822-848.

Bodhi, B. (1999). *A Comprehensive Manual of Abhidhamma: The Philosophical Psychology of Buddhism.* Onalaska, WA: Buddhist Publication Society.

Bishop, S. R., Lau, M., Shapiro, S., Carlson, L., Anderson, N. D. & Carmody, J. (2004). Mindfulness: A proposed operational definition. *Clinical Psychological Science Practice,* 11, 230–241.

Buis, T., Anderson, N. D., Carlson, L., et al. (2006). The Toronto mindfulness scale: development and validation. *Journal of Clinical Psychology,* 62, 1445–1467.

Baer, R. A., Smith, G. T., & Allen, K. B. (2004). Assessment of mindfulness by self-report: The Kentucky Inventory of Mindfulness Skills. *Assessment,* 11, 191–206.

Baer, R. A., Smith, G. T., Hopkins, J., Krietemeyer, J., & Toney, L. (2006). Using self-report assessment methods to explore facets of mindfulness. *Assessment,* 13, 27–45.

Baer, R. A., Smith, G. T., & Allen, K. B. (2004). Assessment of mindfulness by self-report: The Kentucky Inventory of Mindfulness Skills. *Assessment,* 11, 191–206.

Barker, J. (1993). *Paradigms: The Business of Discovering the Future.* New York: Harper Business.

Bass R. (2009). *The Bass Handbook of Leadership: Theory, Research, and Managerial Applications.* New York: Free Press.

Bono, J. E., & Judge, T. A. (2003). Self-concordance at work: Toward understanding the motivational effects of transformational leaders. *Academy of Management Journal*, 46, 554–571.

Burns, James MacGregor. (1979). *Leadership*. New York: Harper Collins.

Bass, B. M., & Yammarino, F. J. (1991). Congruence of self and others' leadership ratings of naval officers for understanding successful performance. *Applied Psychology: An International Review*, 40, 437-454.

Berkson, M. A. (2005). Conceptions of self/no-self and modes of connection comparative soteriological structures in classical Chinese thought. *Journal of Religion and Ethics*, 33, 293–331.

Caldwell, C., Bischoff, S.J., & Karri, R. (2002,). The four umpires: A paradigm for ethical leadership. *Journal of Business Ethics*, 36 (1/2), 153–163.

Caldwell, C.L., Ichiho, R. & Anderson, V. (2017). Understanding level 5 Leaders: The ethical perspectives of leadership humility. *Journal of Management Development*, 36 (5), 724-732.

Cardaciotto, L., Herbert, J. D., Forman, E. M., Moitra, E., & Farrow, V. (2008). The assessment of present - moment awareness and acceptance - the Philadelphia Mindfulness Scale. *Assessment*, 15, 204–223.

Carleton, E., Barling, J., & Trivisonno, M. (2017). Leaders' trait mindfulness and transformational leadership: The mediating roles of leaders' positive affect and leadership self-efficacy. *Frontiers of Psychology*, 8, 1752.

Carmody, J., Reed G, Kristeller J., & Merriam P. Mindfulness, spirituality, and health-related symptoms. (2008). *Journal of Psychosomatic Research*, 64, 393–403.

Carmody, J., & Baer, R. A. (2008). Relationships between mindfulness practice and levels of mindfulness, medical and psychological symptoms and well-being in a mindfulness-based stress reduction program. *Journal of Behavioral Medicine*, 31, 23–33.

Carroll, M. (2007). *The Mindful Leader: Ten principles for Bringing Out the Best in Ourselves and Others*. Boston, Trumpeter.

Carver, C. S. & M. F. Scheier. (1998). *On the Self-Regulation of Behavior*. New York: Cambridge University Press.

Carver, C. S., & Scheier, M. F. (2011). Action, affect, multitasking, and layers of control. In *Psychology of Self-Regulation: Cognitive, Affective, and Motivational Processes, 8*, 109-126.

Carson, S. H., & Langer, E. J. (2006). Mindfulness and self-acceptance. *Journal of Rational Emotions and Cognitive Behavorial Therapy*, 24, 29–43.

Cashman, K. (2008). *Leadership from the Inside Out: Becoming a Leader for Life* (2nd ed.). San Francisco: Barrett-Koehler Publishers.

Castelli, P. (2016). Reflective leadership review: a framework for improving organizational performance. *Journal of Management Development*, 35 (2), 217-236.

Chadwick, P., Hember, M., Symes, J., Peters, E., Kuipers, E. & Dagnan, D. (2008). Responding mindfully to unpleasant thoughts and images: Reliability and validity of the Southampton Mindfulness Questionnaire (SMQ) *British Journal of Clinical Psychology*, 47,451–455

Chambers, R., Gullone, E., & Allen, N. B. (2009). Mindful emotion regulation: An integrative review. *Clinical Psychology Review, 29*, 560–572.

Chambers, R., & Allen, N. B. (2008). The impact of intensive mindfulness training on attentional control, cognitive style, and affect. *Cognitive Therapy and Research, 32*, 303–322.

Charles, A.F. (2013). *Mindfulness meditation in The Workplace.* Raleigh, NC: The Mindfulness Meditation Institute.

Chatterjee, A., & Hambrick, D.C. (20017). It's all about me: Narcissistic chief executive officers and their effects on company strategy and performance. *Administrative Science Quarterly, 52* (3), 351-386.

Chatzisarantis, N. L. D., & Hagger, M. S. (2007). Mindfulness and the intention-behavior relationship within the theory of planned behavior. *Personality and Social Psychology Bulletin, 33*, 663–676.

Chiesa, A., Cherniss, C. & Goleman, D. (2001). *The Emotionally Intelligent Workplace.* San Francisco, CA: Jossey-Bass.

Church, A. H. (1997). Managerial self-awareness in high-performing individuals in organizations. *Journal of Applied Psychology, 82*, 281-292.

Chen, G., Gully, S. M., & Eden, D. (2001). Validation of a new general self-efficacy scale. *Organizational Research Methods, 4*, 62-82.

Clawson, J. G. (2006). *Level Three Leadership: getting below the surface.* Upper Saddle River, New Jersey: Prentice Hall.

Clear, James. (2018). *Atomic Habits: An Easy & Proven Way to Build Good Habits and Break Bad Ones.* New York: Anchor.

Collins, J. (2001). *Good to Great: Why Some Companies Make the Leap and Others Don't.* New York Harper.

Cooper, R. K. & Sawaf, A. (1997). *Executive EQ: Emotional Intelligence in Leadership and Organizations.* New York: Berley Publishing.

Covey, S.R., (1991). *Principle Centered Leadership.* New York: Fireside.

Creed, W.E.D. and Miles, R.E. (1996). Trust in Organizations: A Conceptual Framework Linking Organizational Forms, Managerial Philosophies, and the Opportunity Costs of Controls. In R. M. Kramer & T. R. Tyler (Eds.), *Trust in Organizations: Frontiers of Theory and Research,* pp. 16–38. *Thousand Oaks, CA: Sage.*

Crescentini, C., & Capurso, V. (2015). Mindfulness meditation and explicit and implicit indicators of personality and self-concept changes. *Frontiers in Psychology,* 6, 44.

Damasio, A. (2010). *Self Comes to Mind: Constructing the Conscious Brain.* New York, NY: Pantheon Books.

Dambrun, M., & Ricard, M. (2011). Self-centeredness and selflessness: a theory of self-based psychological functioning and its consequences for happiness. *Review of General. Psychology,* 15, 138–157.

Davidson, R. J. (2010). Empirical explorations of mindfulness: Conceptual and methodological conundrums. *Emotion,* 10, 8–11.

Davis, K.M., Lau, M.A., & Cairns, D.R. (2009). Development and preliminary validation of a trait version of the Toronto Mindfulness Scale. *Journal of Cognitive Psychotherapy: An International Quarterly,* 23,185–197.

Davis, M.H. (1980). A multidimensional approach to individual differences in empathy. *JSAS Catalog of selected documents in psychology*, 10, 85.

Decety, J., & Chaminade, T. (2003). When the self represents the other: A new cognitive neuroscience view on psychological identification. *Consciousness and Cognition*, 12, 577–596.

De Dea Roglio, K., & Light G. (2009). Executive MBA programs: The development of the reflective executive. *Academy of Management Learning & Education*, 8 (2), 156-173.

De Greck, M., Wang, G., Yang, X., Wang, X., Northoff, G., & Han, S. (2012). Neural substrates underlying intentional empathy. *Human Brain Mapping*, 34 (7),135–144.

Deikman, A. J. (1982. *The Observing Self*. Boston, MA: Beacon Press.

Densten, I.L., & Gray, J.H. (2001). Leadership development and reflection: What is the connection? *The International Journal of Educational Management*, 15 (3), 119-125;

DePree, M. (2003). *Leadership is an Art*. New York: Currency Press.

Dickman, M.H., & Stanford-Blair, N. (2009). *Mindful Leadership: A Brain-Based Framework*. Thousand Oaks, CA.: Corwin Press.

Diggins, C. (2004). Emotional intelligence: The key to executive performance. *Human Resource Management*, 12 (1), 33–35.

Dierdorff S., & Rubin, R.S. (March 12, 2015). Research: We're not very self-aware, especially at work, *Harvard Business Review*.

Dierdorff, E.C., Fisher, D.M, & Rubin, R.S. (2019). The power of percipience: Consequences of self-awareness in teams on team-level functioning and performance. *Journal of Management*, 45 (70), 2891-2929.

Dodell-Feder, D., & Tamir, D.I. (2018). Fiction reading has a positive impact on social cognition: A meta-analysis. *Journal of Experimental Psychology*: General, 10, 1037.

Dotlich, D. (2003). *Why CEO's Fail: The 11 Behaviors That Can Derail Your Climb to the Top and How to Manage Them*. San Francisco, CA.: Jossey-Bass.

Donner, S. E. (2010). Self or no self: Views from self-psychology and Buddhism in a postmodern context. *Frontiers of Psychology*, 80, 215–227.

Dunning, D. (2012). *Self-Insight: Roadblocks and Detours on the Path to Knowing Thyself*. N.Y.: Psychology Press

Duval, S. & Wicklund, R.A. (Eds.). (1972). *A Theory of Objective Self-Awareness. New York: Academic Press.*

Duval, T. S. & Lalwani, N. (1999). Objective self-awareness and causal attributions for self-standard discrepancies: Changing self or changing standards of correctness. *Personality and Social Psychology Bulletin*, 25, 1220-1229.

Dreyfus, G. (2011). Is mindfulness present-centered and non-judgmental? A discussion of the cognitive dimensions of mindfulness. *Contemporary Buddhism*, 12, 41–54.

Duhigg, Charles. (2014). *The Power of Habit: Why We Do What We do in Life and Business.* New York: Anchor.

Dutton, J. E., & Heaphy, E. D. (2003). The power of high-quality connections at work. In K. Cameron, J. E. Dutton, & R. E. Quinn (Eds.), *Positive organizational scholarship: Foundations of a new discipline*, pp. 263-278. San Francisco, CA: Berrett-Koehler.

Dutton, K. (2013). *The Wisdom of Psychopaths*. Toronto: Anchor Books.

Dueck, C. (2007). *Mindset: The New Psychology of Success*. New York: Ballantine.

Dulewicz, V., & Higgs, M. (2000). Emotional intelligence: A review and evaluation study. *Journal of Managerial Psychology*, 15 (4), 341-372.

Dunne, J. (2011). Toward an understanding of non-dual mindfulness. *Contemporary Buddhism*, 12, 71–88.

Duval, S., & Wicklund, R. A. (1972). *A Theory of Objective Self-Awareness*. New York: Academic Press.

Edgar, C. (2009). *Inner Productivity: A Mindful Path to Efficiency and Enjoyment in Your Work*. New York: Cruzado Press.

Egleston, D. Castelli, P.A., & Marx, T. G. (2017). Developing, validating, and testing a model of reflective leadership. *Leadership & Organization Development Journal*, 38 (7), 886-896.

Elrod, D. J. (2013). Of confidence and humility. *Strategy and Finance*, 95, 17–18.

Eurich, T. (2018). What Self-Awareness Is and How to Cultivate It. *Harvard Business Review*, January 4.

Eurich, T. (2017). *Insight: The Surprising Truth About How Others See Us, How We See Ourselves, and Why the Answers Matter More Than We Think*. New York: Currency.

Exline, J., & Geyer, A. (2004). Perceptions of humility: A preliminary study. *Self and Identify*, 3, 95-115.

Exline, J., & Hill, P. (2012). Humility: A consistent and robust predictor of generosity, *The Journal of Positive Psychology*, 15, 208-218.

Evans D. R., Baer, R. A., & Segerstrom, S. C. (2009). The effects of mindfulness and self-consciousness on persistence. *Personality and Individual Differences, 47,* 379–382.

Farb, N.A.S. et al., (2007). Attending to the present: mindfulness meditation reveals distinct neural modes of self-reference. *Social, Cognitive and Affective Neuroscience,* 2 (4), 313–322.

Feldman, G., Hayes, A., Kumar, S., Greeson, J., & Laurenceau, J. P. (2007). Mindfulness and emotion regulation: the development and initial validation of the Cognitive and Affective Mindfulness Scale- Revised (CAMS-R). *Journal of Psychopathology Behavior Assessment,* 29, 177–190.

Fletcher, C., and Bailey, C. (2003). Assessing self-awareness: Some issues and methods. *Journal of Managerial Psychology,* 18 (5), 395–404.

Frostenson, M. (2016). Humility in business: A contextual approach. *Journal of Business Ethics,* 138(1), 91-102.

Furtner, M. R., & Rauthmann, J. F. (2010). Relations between self-leadership and scores on the Big Five. *Psychological Reports, 107,* 339–353.

Furtner, M. R., Rauthmann, J. F., & Sachse, P. (2011). The self-loving self-leader: An examination of the relationship between self-leadership and the Dark Triad. *Social Behavior and Personality: An International Journal,* 39, 369–380.

Furtner, M., et al. (2014). The mindful self-leader: Investigating the relationship between self-leadership and mindfulness. *Journal of Leadership Studies,* 8 (2), 242-248.

Gangestad, S.W. & Snyder, M. (2000). Self-monitoring: appraisal and reappraisal. *Psychological Bulletin,* 126 (4), 530-555.

Gardner, W. L., Avolio, B. J., & Walumbwa, F. (2005). Authentic leadership development: Emergent themes and future directions. In W. L. Gardner, B. J. Mackoff, and B.G. Wenet, G. (Eds.), *The Inner Work of Leaders: Leadership as a Habit of Mind.* New York: AMACOM.

Garland, E.L., Gaylord S.A., & Fredrickson B.L. (2011). Positive reappraisal mediates the stress-reductive effects of mindfulness: an upward spiral process. *Mindfulness, 2* (1), 59–67.

Gatling, A.R, Castelli, P.A., & Cole, M.L. (2013). Authentic leadership: The role of self-awareness in promoting coaching effectiveness. *Asia-Pacific Journal of Management Research and Innovation, 9,* 337-343.

Gelles, D. (2012). *Mindful Work: How Meditation is Changing Business from the Inside Out.* New York, NY.: Houghton Mifflin Harcourt.

George, B. (2014). Developing mindful leaders for the C-suite. *Harvard Business Review,* March 10, available at: https://hbr.org/2014/03/developing-mindful-leaders-for-the-c-suite/

Germer, C.K., Siegel, R.D., & Fulton, P.R. (2005). *Mindfulness and Psychotherapy.* New York: Guilford Press.

Ghattterjee, A., & Hamhrick, D.G. (2007). It's all about me: Narcissistic CEOs and their effects on company strategy and performance. *Administrative Science Quarterly, 52,* 351-386.

Goleman, D., Boyatzis, R. & McKee A. (2002). *Primal Leadership.* Cambridge, MA: Harvard Business School Press.

Goleman, D. (2005), *Emotional Intelligence: Why It Can Matter More Than IQ*. New York: Bantam.

Goleman, D., et al. (2017). *Building Blocks of Emotional Intelligence: Emotional Self-Awareness: A Primer*. Florence, MA.: More Than Sound.

Grant, A. M., Franklin, J., & Langford, P. (2002). The self-reflection and insight scale: A new measure of private self-consciousness. *Social Behavior and Personality*, 30, 821-836.

Hafner, M. (2004). How dissimilar others may still resemble the self: Assimilation and contrast after social comparisons. *Journal of Consumer Psychology*, 6(4), 11-119.

Hall, L. (2013). *Mindful Coaching: How Mindfulness Meditation Can Transform Coaching Practice*. London: Kogan Page.

Hayes, S. C., Strosahl, K. D., & Wilson, K. G. (2003). *Acceptance and Commitment Therapy: An Experiential Approach to Behavior Change*. New York, NY: Guilford Press.

Heatherton, T. F., & Wagner, D. D. (2011). Cognitive neuroscience of self-regulation failure. *Trends in Cognitive Sciences*, 15, 132-139.

Hein, G., & Singer, T. (2008). I feel how you feel but not always: The empathic brain and its modulation. *Current Opinions o. Neurobiology*, 18, 153–158.

Herrigel, E. *Zen in the Art of Archery*. (1953). New York: McGraw-Hill.

Holliday, R. *Ego is the Enemy*. (2016). London, UK: Profile Books.

Hougaard, R., et al. (2017). Mindfulness as substitute for transformational leadership. *Journal of Managerial Psychology,* 32 (4), 284-297.

Houghton, J. D., & Neck, C. P. (2002). The revised Self-Leadership Questionnaire: Testing a hierarchical factor structure for self-leadership. *Journal of Managerial Psychology, 17,* 672–691.

Ickes, W. J., Wicklund, R. A., & Ferris, C. B. (1973). Objective self-awareness and self-esteem. *Journal of Experimental Social Psychology, 9,* 202-219.

Josselson, R. (1994). The theory of identity development and the question of intervention: An introduction. In S. L. Archer (Ed.), *Interventions for Adolescent Identity Development.* Thousand Oaks, CA: Sage Publications, pp. 12–25.

Jun, J. (2007). The self in the social construction of organizational reality: Eastern and Western views. *Administrative Theory & Praxis,* 27 (1), 86–111.

Kabat-Zinn J. (1994). *Wherever You Go There You Are: Mindfulness meditation in everyday life.* New York, NY: Hyperion.

Kabat-Zinn, J. (2005). *Coming to Our Senses: Healing Ourselves and the World through Mindfulness.* United Kingdom: Hachette.

Kark, R., & Van-Dijk, D. (2007). Motivation to lead, motivation to follow: The role of the self-regulatory focus in leadership processes. *Academy of Management Review, 32,* 500-528.

Kethledge, R.M., & Erwin, M.S. (2017). *Lead Yourself First: Inspiring Leadership Through Solitude.* New York: Bloomsbury.

Koole, S., Dornan, T., Aper, L., Scherpbier, A., Valcke, M., Cohen-Schotanus, J., & Derese, A. (2011). Factors confounding the assessment of reflection: A critical review. *BMC Medical Education, 11*, 104-116.

Leary, M. R., & Buttermore, N. E. (2003). Evolution of the human self: Tracing the natural history of self-awareness. *Journal for the Theory of Social Behavior, 33*, 365-404.

Leary, M.R. & Banker, C.C. (2020). *A Critical Examination and Reconceptualization of Humility.* New York: Oxford University Press.

Lippincott, M. (2018). Deconstructing the relationship between mindfulness meditation and leader effectiveness. *Leadership & Organization Development Journal, 39*(5), 650-664.

Looman, M.D. (2003). Reflective leadership: Strategic planning from the heart and soul. *Consulting Psychology Journal: Practice and Research, 55*(4), 215-222.

Mackoff, B., & Wenet, G. (2001). *The inner work of leaders: Leadership as a habit of mind.* New York: AMACOM.

McDaniel, E.A., & DiBella-McCarthy, H. (2012). Reflective leaders become causal agents of change. *Journal of Management Development, 31* (7), 663-671.

Mele, A. R. (2001). *Self-Deception Unmasked.* Princeton NJ: Princeton University Press.

Moen, F., & Allgood, E. (2009). Coaching and the effect on self-efficacy. *The Organization Development Journal, 4*, 69-82.

Morin, A. (2011). Self-awareness part 1: Definition, measures, functions, and antecedents. *Social and Personality Psychology Compass, 5*(10), 807-823.

Morin, A., (2011). Self-awareness part 2: Neuroanatomy and importance of inner states. *Speech Journal of Occupational and Organizational Psychology,* 5 (12), 1011-1017.

Morris, J.A. et al. (2005). Bringing humility to leadership: Antecedents and consequences of leader humility. *Human Relations,* 59 (10), 1323-1350.

Moshavl, D., F. W. Brown, F.W., & N. G. Dodd, N.G., (2003). Leader self-awareness and its relationship to subordinate attitudes and performance. *Leadership & Organization Development Journal,* 24 (7/8), 407–418.

Murphy, S. E. (1992). *The contribution of leadership experience and self-efficacy to group performance under evaluation apprehension.* Unpublished doctoral dissertation, University of Washington, Seattle, WA.

Neal, D.T., Wood W., Labrecque, J.S., & Lally, P. (2012). How do habits guide behavior? Perceived and actual triggers of habits in daily life. *Journal of Experimental and Social Psychology,* 48, 492–498.

Nielsen, R., Marrone, J.A., & Slay, H.S. (2009). A new look at humility: Exploring the humility concept and its role in socialized Charismatic Leadership. *Journal of Leadership & Organizational Studies,* 17 (1), 33-43.

Oc, B., Bashshur, M. R., Daniels, M. A., Greguras, G. J., & Diefendorff, J. M. (2015). Leader humility in Singapore. *Leadership Quarterly,* 26, 68–80.

Olendzki, A. (2006). The transformative impact of non-self. In Nauriyal D. K., Drummond M. S., & Lal Y. B. (Eds.), *Buddhist Thought and Applied Psychological Research: Transcending the Boundaries*, New York, NY: Routledge; pp. 50–261

Ostafin, B. D., Robinson M. D., & Meier B. P. (2015). *Handbook of Mindfulness and Self-Regulation.* New York, NY: Springer.

Ou, A. Y., Tsui, A. S., Kinicki, A. J., Waldman, D. A., Xiao, Z., & Song, L. J. (2014). Humble chief executive officers' connections to top management team integration and middle managers' responses. *Administrative Science Quarterly*, 59, 34–72

Ou, A. Y., Waldman, D. A., & Peterson, S. J. (2015). Do humble CEOs matter? An examination of CEO humility and firm outcomes. *Journal of Management*, 44, 1147–1173

Owens, B. P., & Hekman, D. R. (2012). Modeling how to grow: an inductive examination of humble leader behaviors, contingencies, and outcomes. *Academy of Management Journal*, 55, 787–818.

Owens, B. P., & Hekman, D. R. (2016). How does leader humility influence team performance? Exploring the mechanisms of contagion and collective promotion focus. *Academy of Management Journal*, 59, 1088–1111.

Owens, B. P., Johnson, M. D., & Mitchell, T. R. (2013). Expressed humility in organizations: implications for performance, teams, and leadership. *Organization Science*, 24, 1517–1538.

Passmore, J., & Amit, S. (2017). *Mindfulness meditation at Work: The Practice and Science of Mindfulness meditation for Leaders, Coaches and Facilitators.* New York, NY: Nova Science.

Passmore, J. (2019). Mindfulness meditation at organizations (part 1): A critical literature review. *Industrial & Commercial Training*, 2018-0063.

Qian, J., Li, X., Song, B., Wang, B., Wang, M., Chang, S., et al. (2018). Leader's expresses humility and followers' feedback seeking: the mediating effects of perceived image cost and moderating effects of power distance orientation. *Frontiers of Psychology*, 9:563.

Rego, A., Cunha, M. P. E., & Simpson, A. V. (2016). The perceived impact of leaders' humility on team effectiveness: an empirical study. *Journal of Business Ethics*, 148, 205–218

Rego, A., Owens, B., Yam, C. K., Bluhm, D., Cunha, M. P., Silard, A., et al. (2017). Leader humility and team performance: exploring the mediating mechanisms of team psychological capital and task allocation effectiveness. *Journal of Management*, 45, 1009–1033

Ryan, R. M., & Rigby, C. S. (2015). *Did the Buddha Have a self? Handbook of Mindfulness: Theory, Research, and Practice.* New York, NY: Guilford Press.

Sadler-Smith, E. and Shefy, E. (2007). Developing intuitive awareness in management education. *Academy of Management Learning and Education*, 6 (2), 186-205.

Sanford, D. H. (1988). Self-Deception as Rationalization in B. P. McLaughlin and A. O. Rorty (Eds.), *Perspectives on Self-Deception*, Berkeley, CA: University of California Press, pp. 157–169.

Schein, E.H. and Schein, P.A. (2018). Humble Leadership: *The Power of Relationships, Openness and Trust*. Oakland, CA: Berrett-Koehler.

Showry, M., & Manasa, K.V.L. (2014). Self-awareness-key of effective leadership. *The IUP Journal of Soft Skills*, 15 (4), 25-28.

Smith, J. M., & Alloy, L. B. (2009). A roadmap to rumination: a review of the definition, assessment, and conceptualization of this multifaceted construct. *Clinical Psychology Review*, 29, 116–128.

Sosik, J. J., & Megerian, L. E. (1999). Understanding leader emotional intelligence and performance the role of self-other agreement on transformational leadership perceptions. *Group & Organization Management*, 24 (3), 367-390.

Storr, A. (1988). *Solitude: A Return to the Self*. New York: Free Press.

Tang, Y.Y., Hölzel, B.K., & Posner, M.I. (2015). The neuroscience of mindfulness meditation. *Nature Reviews Neuroscience*, 16 (4), 213–225.

Tangey, J.P. (2005). Humility. In *Handbook of Positive Psychology*, (Ed.). C. R. Snyder and S.J. Lopez, pp. 411-410. New York: Oxford University Press.

Taylor, S.N. (2010). Redefining leader self-awareness by integrating the second component of self-awareness. *Journal of Leadership Studies*, 3 (4), 57–68.

Trapnell, P. D., & Campbell, J. D. (1999). Private Self-Consciousness and the Five-Factor Model of Personality: Distinguishing Rumination from Reflection. *Journal of Personality Social Psychology*, 76, 284-304.

Tzu, Lao. (2006). *Tao te Ching.* Trans. Stephen Mitchell. New York: Harper.

Vago, D.R., & Nakamura, V. (2011). Selective attentional bias towards pain-related threat in fibromyalgia: Preliminary evidence for effects of mindfulness meditation training. *Cognitive Therapy and Research,* 35 (6), 581-594.

Vago, D. R., & David, S. A. (2012). Self-awareness, self-regulation, and self-transcendence (S-ART): a framework for understanding the neurobiological mechanisms of mindfulness. *Frontiers of Human Neuroscience,* 6, 296-323.

Van Velsor, E., & Leslie, J. B. (1995). Why executives derail: Perspectives across time and cultures. *Academy of Management Executive,* 9 (4), 62 – 72.

Varela, F. J., Thompson, E., & Rosch, E. (1991). *The Embodied Mind.* Cambridge, MA: MIT Press.

Vera, D., & Rodriquez-Lopez, A. (2001). Strategic virtues: Humility as a source of competitive advantage. *Organizational Dynamics,* 33(4), 393-408.

Wallace, B. A. (2006). *The Attention Revolution.* Sommerville, MA: Wisdom Publications, Inc.

Wang, Y., Liu, J., & Zhu, Y. (2018a). How does humble leadership promote follower creativity? The roles of psychological capital and growth need strength. *Leadership and Organizational Development Journal,* 39, 507–521.

Wang, Y., Liu, J., & Zhu, Y. (2018). Humble leadership, psychological safety, knowledge sharing, and follower creativity: a cross-level investigation. *Frontiers of Psychology,* 9:1727

Wang, L., Owens, B. P., Li, J., & Shi, L. (2018). Exploring the affective impact, boundary conditions, and antecedents of leader humility. *Journal of Applied Psychology*, 103, 1019–1038.

Wexl, K. N., Alexander, R. A, Greenawalt, J. P. & Couch, M. A. (1980). Attitudinal congruence and similarity as related to interpersonal evaluations in manager-subordinate dyads. *Academy of Management Journal*, 23 (2), 320-330.

Whetten, D. A. & Cameron, K.S. (2007). *Key Dimensions of Self-Awareness in Developing Management Skills*. 7th Edition. Upper Saddle River, NJ: Prentice Hall.

White, S. L. (1988). Self-deception and responsibility for the self. In B. P. McLaughlin and A. O. Rorty (Eds.), *Perspectives on Self-Deception.* Berkeley, CA: University of California Press, pp. 450–484.

Whiteside, D.B., & Barclay, L.J. (2016). The face of fairness: Self-awareness as a means to promote fairness among managers with low empathy. *Journal of Business Ethics*, 137, 721-730.

Williams, J. M. G., & Kabat-Zinn J. (2011). Mindfulness: diverse perspectives on its meaning, origins, and multiple applications at the intersection of science and dharma. *Contemporary Buddhism*, 12, 1–18.

Williams, R. (2017). Why great leaders have a coach behind them. *The Financial Post*, May 23, 2014.

Williams, R. (2010). Why CEOs fail and what to do about It. *Financial Post*, July 21.

Williams, R. (2011). Today's Workplace Needs Mindful Leaders. *Financial Post*, April 27.

Williams, R. (2011). A Time for Quiet Leadership. *Financial Post*, January 4.

Williams, R. (2012). Are Organizations Choosing Leaders Lacking Emotional Intelligence? *Financial Post*, July 26.

Williams, R. (2018). 7 Ways Solitude Can Actually Help You. *Fulfillment Daily*, March 6.

Wood, A. W. (1988). Self-Deception and Bad Faith. In B. P. McLaughlin and A. O. Rorty (Eds.), *Perspectives on Self-Deception*. Berkeley, CA: University of California Press, pp. 207–227.

Wood, W. (2013). How do people adhere to goals when willpower is low? The profits (and pitfalls) of strong habits. *Journal of Personality and Social Psychology, 104*, 959–975.

Wood, W., & Neal D.T. (2007). A new look at habits and the habit-goal interface. *Psychological Review*, 114 (4), 843–863.

Wyland, S. C., Inati, S., & Heatherton, T.F. (2002) Finding the self? An event-related fMRI study. *Journal of Cognitive Neuroscience*, 14 (5), 785–794.

Yammarino, F.J., & Atwater, IE. (1997). Do managers see themselves as others see them? Implications of self-other rating agreement for human resources management. *Organizational Dynamics*, 25, 35-44.

Yukl, G. & Mahsud, R. (2010). Why flexible and adaptive leadership is essential. *Consulting Psychology Journal: Practice and Research*, 62 (2), 81-93.

Yukl, G. (2008). How leaders influence organizational effectiveness. *The Leadership Quarterly*, 19 (6), 708-722.

———

Xiao, Q., et al. (2016). The mindful self: A mindfulness-enlightened self-view. *Frontiers of Psychology*, 8, 1752.

Zaccaro, S.J., Foti, R.J. & Kenny, D.A. (1991). Self-monitoring and trait-based variance in leadership: An investigation of leader flexibility across multiple group situations. *Journal of Applied Psychology*, 76(2), 308-315.

Zaccaro, S.J., Gilbert, J.A., Thor, K.K. & Mumford, M.D. (1991). Leadership and social intelligence: Linking social perceptiveness and behavioral flexibility to leader effectiveness. *The Leadership Quarterly*, 2 (4), 317-342.

Zhou, F., & Yenchun, J.W. (2018). How humble leadership fosters employee innovation behavior: A two-way perspective on the leader-employee interaction. *Leadership & Organization Development Journal*, 15, 1-25.

Appendix A

Examples of Self Reflective Questions

1. Am I living true to myself?
2. Am I thinking negative thoughts before I fall asleep?
3. Am I putting enough effort into my relationships?
4. Am I taking care of myself physically?
5. Am I letting matters that are out of my control stress me out?
6. Am I achieving the goals that I've set for myself?
7. Who am I, really?
8. What worries me most about the future?
9. If this were the last day of my life, would I have the same plans for today?
10. What am I really scared of?
11. Am I holding on to something I need to let go of?
12. What matters most in my life?
13. What am I doing about the things that matter most in my life?
14. What have I given up on?
15. When did I last push the boundaries of my comfort zone?
16. If I had to instil one piece of advice in a newborn baby's mind, what advice would I give?
17. What small act of kindness was I once shown that I will never forget?\What do I need to change about myself?
18. How many of my friends would I trust with my life?

19. Who has had the greatest impact on my life?

20. Would I break the law to save a loved one?

21. What do I want most in life?

22. What is life asking of me?

23. How do I define success and failure?

24. What self-less acts have I done to help others lately?

25. What's the one thing I'd like others to remember about me at the end of my life?

26. How much do I worry about what people think of me or what I do?

27. The words I'd like to live by are . . .

28. When I'm in pain—physical or emotional—the kindest thing I can do for myself is…

29. What does unconditional love or acceptance look like for you?

30. I really wish others knew this about me . . .

31. Name a compassionate way you've supported a friend recently. Then, write down how you can do the same for yourself.

32. What always brings tears to your eyes? (As Paulo Coelho has said, "Tears are words that need to be written.")

33. Using only 10 words, describe yourself.

34. What can you learn from your biggest mistakes?

35. Make a list of everything that inspires you—whether books, websites, quotes, people, paintings, stores, or stars in the sky.

36. I feel happiest in my life when . . .

37. Make a list of everything you'd like to say no to.

38. If you had your life to live over again, what would you do differently?

Appendix B

A Sample Self-Awareness Assessment

1. When you make a mistake to what extent has it tended to disrupt your day?
2. How difficult has it been for you to accept the fact that you were not as good at something as you thought you were?
3. How difficult has it been for you to cope with situations that forced you to see yourself in a different way?
4. How important has it been for you to receive praise from others?
5. How often do you compare your standards to those of others?
6. How often do you criticize your own work?
7. How often do you feel guilty when you have not performed to standards?
8. How often do you question your abilities?
9. How often do you reflect on your performance standards after a failure?
10. How often do you compare your performance to the performance of others?
11. How often do you assess whether you "belong" in a given situation?
12. How often has an emotional or difficult situation caused you to reassess your strengths and weaknesses?

13. To what extent do you understand how your characteristics and your experiences have led to you to become the person you are today

14. To what extent do you understand how your personal characteristics lead to your behavior in different situations?

15. To what extent do you use diverse perspectives to arrive at new conclusions about yourself?

16. To what extent would your friends describe you as someone who knows themselves well?

17. After a major accomplishment how likely are you to sit back and enjoy the moment?

18. How often do you know what qualities you bring to a relationship?

19. How often do you modify your standards in order to improve performance?

20. When working on a project, how often can you tell in advance what part would be the easiest for you?

21. To what extent would you say that you consciously think about the ways your thoughts and emotions influence your behavior?

22. How likely are your friends to describe you as introspective?

23. How often did you spend time alone in high school so you could have time to think?

24. How often do you enjoy time alone because it allows you to reflect on your day's activities?

25. How often do you set time aside to reflect on your day?

26. How often do you ponder over how to improve yourself from knowledge of previous experiences?

27. I integrate information about myself from different sources to better understand myself?

28. I often find myself searching internally for explanations of my behavior and emotions?

29. How frequently have the outcomes of your behavior in a given situation caused you to reach an "a-ha" moment about yourself?

30. Relative to your friends, how much time do you spend trying to understand yourself?

31. Relative to your friends, how much time do you spend thinking about the reasons for your behaviors?

Appendix C

Self-Reflective Exercises

Self-Awareness Worksheet

This worksheet is a treasure trove of exercises and ideas to help you think about yourself, including your talents, qualities, values, and perceptions. The point of this worksheet is to help you know and understand:

Finish the Sentence

- I do my best when . . .
- I struggle when . . .
- I am comfortable when . . .
- I feel stress when . . .
- I am courageous when . . .
- One of the most important things I learned was . . .
- I missed a great opportunity when . . .
- One of my favorite memories is . . .
- My toughest decisions involve . . .
- Being myself is hard because . . .
- I can be myself when . . .
- I wish I were more . . .
- I wish I could . . .
- I wish I would regularly . . .

———
199

- I wish I had . . .
- I wish I knew . . .
- I wish I felt . . .
- I wish I thought . . .
- I am going to make my life about. . .

Appendix D

Mindfulness Assessment

- I find it easy to concentrate on what I am doing.
- I can tolerate emotional pain.
- I can accept things I cannot change.
- I can usually describe how I feel at the moment in considerable detail.
- I am easily distracted.
- It's easy for me to keep track of my thoughts and feelings.
- I try to notice my thoughts without judging them.
- I am able to accept the thoughts and feelings I have.
- I am able to focus on the present moment.
- I am able to pay close attention to one thing for a long period of time.
- When I notice an absence of mind, I gently return to the experience of the here and now.
- I accept unpleasant experiences.
- In difficult situations, I can pause without immediately reacting.
- I experience moments of inner peace and ease, even when things get hectic and stressful.
- I notice changes in my body, such as whether my breathing slows down or speeds up.
- I'm good at finding the words to describe my feelings

- I drive on "automatic pilot" without paying attention to what I'm doing.
- When I'm reading, I focus all my attention on what I'm reading.
- I notice how foods and drinks affect my thoughts, bodily sensations, and emotions.
- When I do things, I get totally wrapped up in them and don't think about anything else
- When I have a sensation in my body, it's difficult for me to describe it because I can't find the right words.
- I pay attention to sounds, such as clocks ticking, birds chirping, or cars passing
- When I'm working on something, part of my mind is occupied with other topics, such as what I'll be doing later, or things I'd rather be doing
- I notice when my moods begin to change.

Books by This Author

Eye of the Storm: How Mindful Leaders Can Transform Chaotic Workplaces

The Leadership Edge: Strategies to Transform School Systems

Dragon Tamer

Ready, Aim Influence (contributing author)

Systemic Change: Touchstones for the Future School (contributing author)

About the Author

Ray Williams provides executive coaching, speaking and professional consultations services worldwide. He has over 35 years' experience as a Superintendent of Schools, CEO, senior HR executive, management consultant, trainer, executive coach, professional speaker and author. He has received his undergraduate and graduate training in History, English, Psychology and Organizational Leadership. He is a Certified Master Executive Coach and Certified Hypnotherapist.

Ray is currently President and CEO of Ray Williams Associates, an executive coaching firm based in Vancouver, providing coaching and mentoring to executives in the public and private sectors worldwide. He also is an associate of Virtus Inc., a leadership development company based in Vancouver.

Ray is past president of the International Coach Federation in Vancouver, and held several board positions professional associations in North America. In addition, he has served as a director and Vice-Chair for the Vancouver Board of Trade and director for several community organizations.

Ray's clients have included Fortune 500 companies, the Best Managed Companies in Canada, and dozens of small businesses and entrepreneurial start-ups. Ray has been recognized as one of the top C-Suite coaches in Canada.

Ray has written extensively about leadership, the workplace, organizations, personal development, and social issues including two books on leadership; contributed to several books organizational issues; a novel and screenplay; and been interviewed or written articles for national publications and the media such as *The Financial Post, The Washington Post, Entrepreneur, The Globe and Mail,* the *Vancouver Sun, USA Today* and *Inc.,* and online media such as *Psychology Today, Fulfillment Daily, Business.com and Medium.* He has written two previous books on leadership, *The Leadership Edge,* and was a contributing author to *Ready, Aim, Influence.* In addition, he has written a novel, *Dragon Tamer.*

His latest book, *Eye of the Storm: How Mindful Leaders Can Transform Chaotic Workplaces,* which looks at how mindful leaders can make a big difference to organizational success and employee well being.

Beyond his professional training and experience, Ray brings his insights into human behavior, having been born and raised in Hong Kong, where his family were imprisoned for four years by the Japanese in WWII, which allows him a unique perspective on overcoming adversity, and sustaining a positive outlook.

CPSIA information can be obtained
at www.ICGtesting.com
Printed in the USA
LVHW081946190520
656072LV00009B/922